The
Little Dictionary
Of
Gender Identity

Published by Lanx Satura Publishing, Maine
Printing and distribution by Lulu Press, North Carolina.
Worldwide printing and distribution by Ingram Press.

ISBN: 978-1-716-07216-1

Contact the publisher and authors for all comments, additions, sales inquires:
P.O. Box 15382, Portland, Maine 04112 USA
aronmatyas@hotmail.com

This book dedicated to the late Harvey Milk and all who who have given their lives.

My writing partner Dr. Faustus shared a news article with me that said there were over 100 gender identities. As a lesbian he was curious as to my opinion. In looking for that list online we found there were many lists, ranging from 3 to well over 100 genders. We found some lists included only genders recognized by current science. Elsewhere folx with genders outside of official recognition status would be asking on forums why they were being excluded. Why was one gender better or more legit than another? This made us curious, so we kept digging and found the lists didn't always overlap.

We decided to help the conversation move to a higher ground by creating this dictionary of every gender identity we could find. I am part of the gender conversation. Growing up in an age where Ellen had not yet come out on TV I didn't have resources like the internet or this book. People were not so accepting of differences. I wasn't male nor female nor Trans. For much of my life I was told I was thus "needing therapy." That wasn't the answer either. I have begrudgingly come to identify as Trans, but had I a book like this I might have felt comfortable choosing a better fitting label without fear. We made this for those who are in my shoes. We made this to tell folx not to fear.

Dr. Faustus and I are not scientists or doctors. We claim no final say, superior insight, or anything else. We wanted this book to be small and affordable, thus definitions were streamlined. Yes, that might ruffle some feathers and leave a lot out. Feel free to e-mail us your thoughts on this for a future expanded edition.

The genders listed all use masculine and feminine as the starting point. There are other genders called alignments that use other things, such as crystals, as their foundation. We have not included many of those, while those we did actually use feminine and masculine in some way.

Some genders are more masculine leaning or more feminine leaning, and thus we have marked those with the appropriate binary gender symbol. Everything else is up to interpretation or nonbinary or having no gender.

There might be errors, missing words and other things. We welcome any e-mails and will consider everything for inclusion in a future edition. You can reach us at aronmatyas@hotmail.com.

Dr. Matthew Faustus, D.D. (he/him/his) is a heterosexual Christian minister who worked as an academic advisor at The Interfaith Seminary of Texas. He thought he had an open mind, until he saw the damage President Trump did to America. He saw the open-minded Christians around him weren't any different then closed-minded conservatives. It was all a charade and Dr. Faustus lost his faith. His Christian work focused on personal spiritual growth and mysticism. Now he does holistic life coaching and achieving one's dreams as a healing tool.

Jamie Ray (they/them/theirs) is a non-binary trans activist with the Antifa and BLM movements who self-identifies as a non-queer lesbian. They has guested articles for numerous blogs and magazines, often focusing on finding personal growth and healing via alternative spaces, and working with alternative parenting approaches for raising a sex positive child.

The two met when they both appeared on a panel discussing sexual conversion therapy. This is their second book. Their first, available on Amazon and other online distributors, is 'Rebuilding America: A Liberal Proposal For A Post-Trump Social Revolution To Save America.'

ABANDOE .... Empty and intimidating like an abandoned house, might be genderless.

ABIGENDERT .... Two distinct non-neutral genders simultaneously or separately but only feeling loose or vague connections to them.

ABIMEBOY ♂ .... Masculine variation of Abimegender.

ABIMEGENDER .... Profound, deep, infinite, like a mirror reflecting a mirror. {Abimeboy, Abimegirl}

ABIMEGIRL ♀ .... Feminine variation of abimegender.

ABINARY (Exterbinary, Offbinary) .... Changes binary genders into nonbinary gender.

ABOIXYGENDER ♂♀ .... Three genders with Abinary then boy then girl.

ABSORGENDER .... Fluid, being the gender of all the people around one's self until a single gender is taken for the moment.

ACEAROGENDER (Aroacegender, A-Spec, A-Spectrum) .... On aromantic and asexual spectrum.

ACECORIC .... Connected to pride in being asexual.

ACEGENDER .... Where being ace is so intertwined to one's gender the two can't be separated.

ACHILLEANGENDER (Gaygender, Vinciangender) ♂ .... A masculine gender attracted to men where gender and sexuality are completely intertwined.

ACHILLEGENDER ♂ .... Only experiencing masculinity through one's attraction to men or male oriented genders.

ACTABAONIC .... Like on holiday but moving to new holiday locations when looked for.

ADAMASGENDER .... A gender refusing to be categorized.

ADHDgender .... Connected to one's ADHD.

ADHDnurix .... Connected to one's attention deficiency and hyperactivity due to ADHD, like gender is hidden behind brain fog.

ADnurix.......... Connected to one's attention deficiency due to ADHD, might be like gender is hidden in a brain fog.

ADUSTUSGENDER .... Charred around the edges.

ADVENABOY (Advenaman, Advenamasculine) ♂ .... Masculine variation of Advenagender.

ADVENAFEMININE (Advenagirl, Advenawoman) ♀ .... Feminine variation of Advenagender

ADVENAGENDER .... Intersex, struggle to identify as assigned gender at birth due to feeling alienated from it. {Advenaboy, Advenafeminine, Advenagirl, Advenaman, Advenamasculine, Advenawoman}

ADVENAGIRL (Advenawoman; see Advenafeminine) ♀

ADVENAMAN (Advenamasculine; see Advenaboy) ♂

ADVENAMASCULINE (Advenaman; see Advenaboy) ♂

ADVENAWOMAN (Advenagirl; see Advenafeminine) ♀

ADVENTURECORIC .... Connected to feelings of adventure or things connected to adventure, or like adventurous feelings.

AECORISGENDER .... Feels sunk in an ocean but at some point bobs up.

AELDARIAN (Ailderian) ♂ .... Bad ass, strongly masculine.

AEROGENDER .... Fluid and connected to one's surroundings, might change in response to different surroundings.

AEROSOLGENDER .... Connected to mist, particles, like floating particles rather than something whole, might feel dissociation.

AESIGENDER .... Stylish, trendy.

AESSOLUM .... Connected to wealth, freedom, self-control, color bronze.

AESTHETGENDER (Aestheticgender, Aesthetigender, Videgender) .... Connected to an aesthetic.

AESTHETICGENDER (Aesthetigender, Videgender; see Aesthetgender)

AESTHETIFLUX .... Fluid between Aesthetgenders.

AESTHETIGENDER (Aestheticgender, Videgender; see Aesthetgender)

AETHERBOY ♂ .... Masculine variation of Aethergender.

AETHERGENDER .... Very wide, commanding, breathtaking, powerful, might be connected to the vast expanse of space. {Aetherboy, Aethergirl}

AETHERGIRL ♀ .... Feminine variation of Aethergender.

AFAB (Assigned Female At Birth) ♀ .... Assigned female at birth.

AFEMIGENDER (Afeminigender, Afeminogender, Efemigender, Efeminigender, Effeminigender, Effeminogender, Ginandrigender, Ginandrogender, Gynandrigender, Gynandrogender) ♂♀ .... Masculine with effeminate presentation, might not identify female.

AFEMINIGENDER (Afeminogender, Efemigender, Efeminigender, Effeminigender, Effeminogender, Ginandrigender, Ginandrogender, Gynandrigender, Gynandrogender; see Afemigender) ♂♀

AFEMINOGENDER (Afeminigender, Efemigender, Efeminigender, Effeminigender, Effeminogender, Ginandrigender, Ginandrogender, Gynandrigender, Gynandrogender; see Afemigender) ♂♀

AFFECTUGENDER .... Connected to mood swings.

AFISGENDER .... Hazy, dreamlike, hard to conceptualize.

AGENDER (Genderfree, Genderless, Non-Gendered) .... No gender identity, might have free sense of gender.

AGENDERFLUIX (Gxnderfluix) .... Predominantly Agender but fluid between other genders.

AGENDERFLUX ♂♀ .... Agender with fluctuating femininity and masculinity.

AGENDERVIR ♂ .... Agender male.

AGEREGENDER (Littlefluid) .... Changing with age regression, entirely, partially or temporarily.

AGGELOS .... Partially soft masculine and feminine presentation with rest being another gender not describable in words, might be connected to delusions of divinity, angelicism.

AILDERIAN (see Aeldarian) ♂

AIMAGENDER .... A gender from seeing one's own blood due to injury.

AISTHESISGENDER .... A gender made of sensations, or is a sensation.

ALBAGENDER .... Being white or white light.

ALBUSOLUM .... Connected to angels, feathers, stars, fae, color white.

ALCOHOLICGENDER .... Connected to one's alcoholism, might change depending on being sober or drinking.

ALEXANDRIDIC .... Changing in color and presentation due to weather.

ALEXIGENDER .... Fluid between multiple genders but one can't fully identify or describe those genders.

ALGAEIX .... A gender effecting many aspects of one's life, might consume one's thoughts due to obsessive tendencies, might drain one's mental health.

ALGIAGENDER .... Changes depending on one's pain levels or type of pain being experienced, due to chronic pain.

ALIAGENDER (Quasixenic, Xenogender) .... Not fitting into existing or traditional gender constructs, might utilize non-human approaches to gender.

ALIENCORIC .... Connected to aliens.

ALIENGENDER .... An interpretation of genders from non-human perspectives, or only describable from non-human perspectives.

ALIQUDCAER .... Only describable as opposites to the point of confusion and stress.

ALIUSGENDER .... A gender removed from common and traditional gender terms.

ALLEKEINEGENDER (Gengender) .... Being all genders and no gender, encompassing every aspect of gender.

ALNILAMFLUID .... Fluid between Nyctogenders.

ALTCORIC .... Connected to an alternative cultural scene.

AY'LONIT ♂♀ .... Jewish, assiged female at birth, Trans.

AMAB (Assigned Male At Birth) ♂ .... Assigned male at birth.

AMALGAGENDER (Amalgender, Integender, Mera) .... Connected to being intersex.

AMALGENDER (Integender, Mera; see Amalgagender)

AMAREGENDER .... Changing depending on one's love interest.

AMARYLLIAN .... Connected to one's gender fluidity.

AMBIGENDER .... Two genders simultaneously without fluctuation.

AMBONEC ♂♀ .... Both male and female but neither simultaneously. {Amboneith, Ambonekko}

AMBONEITH ♀ .... Feminine variation of Ambonec.

AMBONEKKO ♂ .... Masculine variation of Ambonec.

AMICAGENDER .... Changing depending on which friend one is with.

AMISSOFLUID .... Now lost, unknown, fluid between confusing genders, might be connected to darkness, winter, gloominess.

AMONGUSGENDER .... Connected to video game Among Us.

ANCIENTUS .... Becoming ancient and unused.

ANDROGYNE ♂♀ .... Nonbinary and masculine and feminine, might become neutral.

ANDROGYNOS .... Jewish, Bigender, Androgyne.

ANDROIDGENDER .... Connected to Android characters in video game Detroit Become Human.

ANDROX ♂ .... Between male and Androgyne.

ANEMIAGENDER .... Connected to one's anemia.

ANESIGENDER .... Feeling a certain gender but feeling more comfortable identifying with another.

ANGEGENDER (Hategender) .... Not describable without using hatred or anger, might be due to a mental disorder bringing on negative feelings.

ANGELCORIC .... Connected to angels.

ANGELGENDER .... Connected to character Angel/Experiment 624 of TV show Lilo & Stitch, might be loyal, loving, musical, mischievous, fluid.

ANGENITAL .... A gender desiring to be without primary sexual characteristics without necessarily being Agender.

ANGERCORIC .... Connected to anger, might not be angry.

ANGESOLUM .... Bright, connected to the sun, angels, colors cyan and yellow.

ANGREPROBIC .... Feeling was once holy, strong, powerful, permanently fell into darkness due to trauma, might be religious.

ANIBOY ♂ .... Masculine variation of Anigender.

ANIGENDER (Animecoric, Animegender) .... Connected to Japanese Anime. {Aniboy, Anigirl, Aninonbinary}

ANIGIRL ♀ .... Feminine variation of Anigender.

ANIMALCORIC (Faunagender) .... Connected to animals.

ANIMECORIC (Animegender; see Anigender)

ANIMEGENDER (Animecoric; see Anigender)

ANIMIGENDER .... A gender where one's mental disorder makes it hard to find a gender fitting one's needs.

ANINONBINARY .... Nonbinary variation of Anigender.

ANOBOY ♂ .... Masculine variation of Anogender.

ANOGENDER .... Fading in and out but always coming back to the same feeling. {Anoboy, Anogirl}

ANOGIRL ♀ .... Feminine variation of Anogender.

ANONBINARY .... Neither binary nor nonbinary.

ANONGENDER .... A gender unknown to both one's self and others.

ANOREXGENDER .... Connected to one's anorexia.

ANQUILLE .... Like peaceful sleeping, might be connected to soft light, nostalgia, colors soft brown, earth tones, physical warmth.

ANSGENDER .... Connected to one's ancestors.

ANSIGENDER .... A gender being more correct for one's self, but another gender is more comfortable.

ANTAGENDER .... Connected to villians, antagonists in stories, movies, TV shows, games, might be dark, mischevious, sneaky, sassy, daring, might be sad, lonely, inwardly bitter.

ANTEGENDER .... Potentially can be anything but is formless, motionless, not manifesting as any particular gender.

ANTHEIC .... Being beauty, love, with aesthetics being an important part of the presentation.

ANTIANCIENTIUS .... Like coming back from being ancient and unused to being new and used.

ANTIBINARY .... Opposite of binary, people of color.

ANTIBOY ♀ .... Masculine variation of Antigender.

ANTIFISCIGENDERFLUX .... Weaker when possessing money and assets.

ANTIGENDER .... Only describable as opposite of another gender. {Antiboy, Antigirl}

ANTIGIRL ♂ .... Feminine variation of Antigender.

ANTINONBINARY .... Opposite of nonbinary.

ANTIQUAFACHEON .... Connected to antiques, old fashion things.

ANTIQUAFLUID .... Fluid, eventually solidifies feeling lost in other genders then turns fluid again to be reused.

ANTIQUEASIM .... Feeling antique among genders, like became an older version of itself.

ANTIQUEGENDER .... Connected to antiques, vintage feelings, dusty records, unpolished silver, old toys, might get stronger or grow around antiques.

ANXIEGENDER (Imnigender) .... Connected to one's anxiety, might fluctuate with changes in anxiety.

APAGENDER .... Apathetic towards one's gender and not caring enough to investigate further.

APCONSUGENDER .... One knows what it isn't but not what it is as it appears to be hiding.

APHRODISIAN (Bigenital, Salmacian) ♂♀ .... Male or female to intersex transsexuals.

APOGENDER .... A gender entirely removed from concepts of gender.

APORAGENDER .... Having strong nonbinary identification.

APORAVIR .... Part male and part Aporagender.

APREMASEINE ♂ .... Agender but comfortable with masculinity.

APRILIEAN .... Calm, flowing, flowery, springy, upbeat, might be connected to flower gardens, parks, sunshine, spring.

AQUARIGENDER (Genderflow) .... Fluid gender perpetually changing, never able to be categorized as a specific gender, might not have set number of genders it flows between.

AQUAGENDER .... Connected to color aqua.

ARCAGE .... Desolate, unused, like its locked up in a coffin or mausoleum, might be connected to Halloween, cemeteries.

ARCHAIBOY ♂ .... Masculine variation of Archaigender.

ARCHAICGENDER .... A gender stretching far beyond one's age or lifetime.

ARCHAIGENDER .... Ancient, old, big. {Archaiboy, Archaigirl, Archainonbinary}

ARCHAIGIRL ♀ .... Feminine variation of Archaigender.

ARCHAINONBINARY .... Nonbinary variation of Archaigender.

ARDORIAN ♀ .... Warm, like flame, fluctuates with other genders.

ARGESOLUM .... Connected to silence, the moon, rocks, technology, color silver.

AROACEGENDER (A-Spec, A-Spectrum; see Acearogender)

AROGENDER .... Connected by one's place on aromatic spectrum.

AROMAGENDER .... Connected to scents, like the scent replaces the gender.

ARROYAN .... Like a small creak or stream.

ARSENOGENDER ♂ .... Masculine gender altered by toxic masculinity, might have conflicting feelings on one's masculinity, might not feel connected to masculinity.

ARTCORIC .... Connected to art, might have an artistic presentation and create art or just be interested in and surrounded by art.

ARTHURGENDER .... Connected to heroes in stories, movies, shows, comics, might be strong, brave, secretly, insecure, scared to lose.

ARTISTIANGENDER .... Connected to being an artist of any medium.

A-SPEC (Aroacegender, A-Spectrum; see Acearogender)

A-SPECTRUM (Aroacegender, A-Spec; see Acearogender)

ASSIGNED FEMALE AT BIRTH (see AFAB) ♀

ASSIGNED MALE AT BIRTH (see ABAB) ♂

ASTERGENDER .... Bright, celestial.

ASTRALGENDER (Spacecoric, Starfluid) .... Connected to space, might be connected to aliens.

ASTROLLIGENDER .... Connected to concept of gender identity by internet trolls.

ASTRONOGENDER .... Connected to space but not aliens.

ASTROVIR ♂ .... A gender with masculinity central to one's identity.

ATERGENDER .... Deep, dark, intimate.

ATLAGENDER .... Connected to TV show Avatar The Last Airbender.

AUDIOGENDER (Musicgender) .... Only describable through specific music genres, bands, aesthetics.

AURANSOLUM .... Connected to campfires, the moon, warmth, color orange.

AUREUSGENDER .... Ancient, golden, lost.

AURUSOLUM .... Connected to family, suns, comfort, self-identification, color gold.

AUSTUIAN .... Calming like fading out of summer into autumn, might be connected to beaches.

AUTGENDER (Autigender, Antiqueer, Autismgender) .... A gender only understandable by being autistic.

AUTIGENDER (Autiqueer, Autismgender; see Autgender)

AUTIQUEER (Autigender, Autismgender; see Autgender)

AUTISMGENDER Autigender, Autiqueer; see Autgender)

AUTOAIMAGENDER .... A gender from seeing one's own blood due to self-injury.

AUTOGENDER .... A gender deeply personal to oneself but difficult to describe with traditional gender terms.

AUTUMNUSIAN .... Partially neutral, connected to autumn, rain, fallen leaves, oak trees.

AVARUMGENDER .... A gender where one feels many terms might be used none can be identified with due to anxiety, mental disorder.

AVENTUREGENDER .... A gender found my chance, little hazy, brings harmony.

AXAB (Unassigned Gender At Birth) .... Unassigned gender at birth.

AXIGENDER .... Two genders at opposite ends of an axis but experiencing one at a time with no overlap and short transition time.

AZURIC .... A gender contradicting itself, calm, other worldly energy.

BABYCORIC .... Connected to babies, raising babies, might not be connected to parenting.

BACKROOMIC .... Fuzzy feeling of nostalgia, slightly other worldly.

BAGELGENDER .... Connected to bagels, might be connected to Jewish culture.

BALLORAGENDER (Ballorgender, Loragender) .... Connected to character Ballora from video game Five Nights at Freddy's: Sister Location, might be graceful, musical, trapped.

BALLORGENDER (Loragender; see Balloragender)

BAMBIGENDER ♂♀ .... Vulnerable, curious, playful, protective bravery, might be social prey, need to feel overly cautious.

BARBIEGENDER (Barbiegirlsgender, BGCgender) .... Connected to video game barbiegirls.com, might be connected to Barbie toys.

BARBIEGIRLSGENDER (BGCgender; see Barbiegender)

BATHGENDER .... Warm, comforting, like a peaceful bubble bath.

BATIMgender (Bendyandtheinkmachinegender) .... Connected to game Bendy And The Ink Machine.

BEACHCORIC .... Connected to beaches.

BEARIC .... Connected to character Fredbear of video game Five Nights At Freddy's, might be original, old, musical, slightly dangerous, mechanical.

BELLAGENDER (Cutegender, Gendercute) .... Connected to being cute.

BELTZAAIN .... Connected to color black, might be connected to night, the moon, space, darkness.

BENDYANDTHEINKMACHINEGENDER (see BATIMgender)

BERRYCORIC .... Connected to berries.

BESTOWGENDER (Prezgender) .... A gender that exists or changes when receiving gifts. {Prezboy, Prezgirl}

BETAGENDER .... Like a beta test of another gender.

BGCgender (Barbiegirlsgender; see Barbiegender)

BICORIC ♂♀ .... Connected to bisexuality.

BIGENDER .... Two genders simultaneously or separately.

BIGENTIAL (Salmacian; see Aphrodisian) ♂♀

BIOGENDER (Naturecoric, Naturengender) .... Connected to nature.

BIPOLARGENDER .... Connected to one's bipolar disorder.

BIRL .... Nonbinary, non-stereotypical, boy and girl simultaneously, might only be in one's gender presentation, might be androgynous.

BI-VIR (Malinegender) ♂ .... Two male genders simultaneously or separately.

BLADEGENDER .... Like a bladed weapon, might not be sharp, dangerous.

BLANKETGENDER .... Constantly warm, soft.

BLENIS MISK ♂♀ .... Only feeling masculine when wearing strap-on dildos, might present traditional masculinity when wearing strap-ons.

BLINDGENDER .... Like blindness as one is unable to see and understand the gender as it appears almost invisible.

BLINDNESSGENDER .... Connected to one's partial or complete blindness.

BLUEGENDER .... Connected to color blue.

BLURGENDER (Genderfuzz) .... More than one gender but they are blurred together and can't be individually identified.

BLURISYSGENDER (Calisgender) .... Blurry, hard to recognize.

BOETHIC .... Fluid between a gender and its Antigender.

BOI ♂ .... Nonbinary, people of color.

BONIC (Funtic) .... Connected to character Funtime Freddy of video game Five Nights At Freddy's, might be crazy, hysterical, party-like, wide awake, mechanical.

BOOKCORIC .... Connected to books, might be connected to writing.

BOQORGEERIGENDER .... Connected to feeling royalty, color purple, might be connected to death.

BORDERFLUID (Bordergender) .... Fluid, connected to one's Borderline Personality Disorder, might lack a firm grasp of one's gender.

BORDERGENDER (see Borderfluid)

BORDERIX .... Connected to one's favorite person due to one's Borderline Personality Disorder, might change in intensity or be non-existent.

BOSGENDER ♂ .... Connected to Texas Longhorn cattle.

BOTGENDER .... Cold, steel, like a robot without emotions.

BOWGENDER .... Shoots the gender forward.

BOYFLUX ♂ .... Feeling mostly or all male most of the time with fluctuating intensities of masculine gender identity.

BRILLANTESOLUM .... Bright, connected to the sun, deserts, color yellow.

BRUISEGENDER (Genderbruised) .... Sensitive, hurting without ability to heal whenever it is explored, might be due to trauma, anxiety, mental disorders.

BRUSOLUM .... Connected to music, books, stars, movies, color brown.

BUGGENDER .... Connected to bugs.

BULLBOY ♂ .... Masculine variation of Bullgender.

BULLGENDER .... Connected to cows. {Bullboy, Bullgirl}

BULLGIRL ♀ .... Feminine variation of Bullgender.

BURLESGENDER (Ziggystardustgender) .... An extremely hard to label gender being flamboyant, fabulously androgynous, might not take itself seriously.

BURSTGENDER .... Coming in intense bursts of feeling then quickly fading back to its original state.

BUSOGENDER .... Connected to busses, might be connected to other types of public transport.

BUSYGENDER .... A gender too busy to have a gender.

BXY ♂ .... Both masculine and no gender simultaneously or separate.

CABLEDABOY ♂ .... Masculine variation of Cabledagender.

CABLEDAGENDER .... Like tangled up in cables, destroyed, potentially short circuiting, might be connected to something bigger. {Cabledaboy, Cabledagirl, Cabledaneutrois}

CABLEDAGIRL ♀ .... Feminine variation of Cabledagender.

CABLEDANEUTROIS .... Neutrois variation of Cabledagender.

CADENSGENDER (Musiccoric) .... Connected to music, might create music or just enjoy it.

CADOANDROGYNE .... Androgynous variation of Cadogender.

CADOBOY ♂ .... Masculine variation of Cadogender.

CADOGENDER .... A gender with a gender to fall back on. {Cadoandrogyne, Cadoboy, Cadogirl, Cadonb}

CADOGIRL ♀ .... Feminine variation of Cadogender.

CADONB .... Nonbinary variation of Cadogender.

CAEDGENDER (Caedogender) .... Being damaged or lessened or lost by trauma.

CAEDOGENDER (see Caedgender)

CAELGENDER .... Like space, stars, nebulas, comets, other intergalactic objects.

CAERSOLUM .... Connected to lakes, rivers, stars, birds, color blue.

CAERULGENDER .... Calming, open-minded, identifying with oceans when the weather is colder and identifying with the sky when the weather is warmer.

CAKECORIC .... Connected to cake.

CALIDUMGENDER .... Like a warm pool of liquid.

CALIDUMIAN .... Warm feeling.

CALISGENDER (see Blurisysgender)

CAMOGENDER .... Hard to see on the outside but full of meaning on the inside.

CAMPINGCORIC .... Connected to camping.

CANDYCORIC (Candyic, Canyic, Souryic) .... Connected to candy.

CANDYIC (Canyic;, Souryic see Candycoric)

CANYIC (Candyic, Souryic; see Candycoric)

CARTAGENDER (Cartegender, Chartagender) .... Connected to playing cards.

CARTEGENDER (Chartagender; see Cartagender)

CASCADAN .... Like a waterfall.

CASSGENDER .... Feeling indifferent to one's gender believing it is not important but still having a gender.

CASTLECORIC .... Connected to castles.

CATBOY ♂ .... Masculine variation of Catgender.

CATGENDER (Kittengender, Kittycoric, Kittygender, Nyagender) .... Connected to cats, might be due to delusions of being a cat due to mental disorders. {Catboy, Catgirl}

CATGIRL ♀ .... Feminine variation of Catgender.

CAUSTIGENDER .... Acidic, gradually dissolves all other genders becoming sole remaining gender.

CAVILEIC .... Connected to trickery, mischief, underlying tone of power, other worldly energy.

CAVUSGENDER .... One gender when depressed and another when not depressed.

CELESTARIAN ♂♀ .... Juparian, Lunettia, Mercurian simultaneously or separate.

CEMETARIAN .... Connected to cemeteries, gravestones, black cats, might be quiet, mysterious, might crumble away to nothing repeatedly.

CENDGENDER .... Changing between one gender and its opposite.

CENRELL ♂ .... Most comfortable within gender neutral spectrum but feeling strong attachments to masculinity.

CERESIAN ♀ .... Plutoian, Lunettian.

CEREUSGENDER .... Barely there, masking something new, beautiful, like candlelight.

CERUL ♀ .... Nonbinary with traditional feminine presentation.

CETEROFLUID ♂♀ .... Fluid Ceterogender.

CETEROGENDER ♂♀ .... A gender with specific masculine or feminine or neutral feelings.

CHAIAN .... Soft, fuzzy, warm, childlike. {Chauceia, Chauxian}

CHALOOUINFLUID (Chaloouingfluix, Genderchaloouin) .... Fluid between Halloween and autumn related genders.

CHALOOUINFLUIX (Genderchaloouin; see Chaloouinfluid)

CHANGELIC .... Feeling stolen, replaced by a gender wearing a disguise.

CHAOSFLUX .... A gender fluid due to one's hormonal disorders.

CHAOTIGENDER .... A gender not properly discovered and analyzed due to ADHD.

CHAOTIQUEER .... Strange, bold, prideful, hard to define, unapologetically visible, unleashes one's queerness, might be connected to anarchy, might blur lines between multiple genders.

CHAOUIAN .... Neutral variation of Chaian.

CHARAGENDER (Egogender, Namegender) .... Solely based on one's self where no words seem to define it other than one's name or saying it is uniquely one's self.

CHARCON .... Like a puddle.

CHARMAGENDER ♀ .... Feminine variation of Charmegender.

CHARMEGENDER .... Magical in nature. {Charmagender, Charmogender}

CHARMOGENDER ♂ .... Masculine variation of Charmegender.

CHARTAGENDER (Cartegender; see Cartagender)

CHAUCEIA ♀ .... Feminine variation of Chaian.

CHAUXIAN ♂ .... Masculine variation of Chaian.

CHEERBEARGENDER .... Nonbinary, connected to fictional character Cheer Bear from 1980's Care Bears cartoon, might be happy, magical, carefree.

CHESHIRIC .... Confusing, easily going invisible, suddenly appearing, like vague riddles.

CHICKENCORIC .... Connected to chickens.

CHOCOYIC .... Connected to chocolate.

CHROMAFLUID .... Having all the beautiful colors in the world.

CHROMAERGENDER .... Changing colors with the environment, seasons, surrounding people, other external factors. {Chromaerxirl, Chromaerxoy}

CHROMAERXIRL ♀ .... Feminine variation of Chromaergender.

CHROMAERXOY ♂ .... Masculine variation of Chromaergender.

CHROMAGENDER (Colorcoric, Colorgender, Colorqueer) .... Connected to one or more colors.

CHROMEGENDER .... Fast, knows everything about one's self.

CINDERSPLOOF .... Connected to fire, warm blankets, poofy and soft things.

CINEMAGENDER .... Connected to cinema, might be connected to Hollywood culture.

CIRCABYGENDER .... Mischevious, soft spoken, antagonistic, malicious, trickful, hidden lingering sadness, might be connected to ice cream, circuses, horror, feeling sweet, melted.

CIRCLEGENDER .... Having feelings of completion, symmetry.

CIRCUSCORIC .... Connected to circuses, clowns, acrobatics, animals, might be connected to darker aspects of circuses.

CIRQUOIBOY ♂ .... Masculine variation of Cirquoigender.

CIRQUOIGENDER .... Whimsical, bizarre, bubbly, silly, social concept of gender is nonsense, not applicable

CIRQUOIGIRL ♀ .... Feminine variation of Cirquoigender.

CISGENDER .... Being the assigned gender at birth all the time.

CITRUSLUSIA .... Goofy, large, might be connected to pumpkins, autumn, Halloween, color orange.

CITYCORIC (Towncoric) .... Connected to towns, cities.

CLAMOSOLUM .... Connected to cameras, eyes, history, color cyan.

CLASSICALGENDER ♂♀ .... Connected to historical definitions and presentations of masculinity or femininity versus pre-2000 interpretations.

CLEANCORIC (Cleangender) .... Connected to cleaning or being clean.

CLEANGENDER (see Cleancoric)

CLIFFNAP .... Exhausted, about to fall asleep.

CLOTHGENDER .... Like soft cloth.

CLOTHIOFLUID .... Fluid, flowing like waves, or a washing machine rhythm.

CLOUDCORIC .... Connected to clouds.

CLOVERGENDER .... Adults who identify as children and are sexually or romantically attracted to children.

CLOWNCORIC (Clowngender) .... Fun, silly, clumsy, color, connected to clowns.

CLOWNGENDER (see Clowncoric)

COASTERGENDER .... Like a rollercoaster with highs, lows, going very fast with sudden restraints.

COBWEBIAN .... Sticky, intermingled, close together, might be connected to spiders, Halloween.

COCODILIC .... Connected to one's levels of empathy, might be misunderstood but genuinely helpful.

CODEGENDER .... Partially or completely composed of digital code.

COEURSOLUM .... Dark, connected to bloodlines, control, creation, color purple.

COEXTA .... A gender with a vague inconsistent relationship to one, might not feel like gender is applicable, might be indescribable gender identity.

COGENDER (Enbie, Gender Nonconforming, Genderqueer, Gender Variant, Nonbinary, Third Gender, X-Gender) .... Not exclusively categorizable as male or female, might be Trans.

COGITOGENDER (Existigender) .... Only existing when one thinks about it, might be quiet until called to attention, might be Agender until a gender is consciously chosen.

COLLGENDER .... Too many genders simultaneously to describe each one.

COLORCORIC (Colorgender, Colorqueer; see Chromagender)

COLORGENDER (Colorcoric, Colorqueer; see Chromasgender)

COLORQUEER (Colorcoric, Colorgender; see Chromagender)

COLUMNFLUID .... Fluid gender changing its height.

COMMOGENDER .... Settling with one's assigned gender at birth for the present time.

COMPUTERCORIC .... Connected to computers.

CONDIGENDER .... Only felt at certain circumstances.

CONPLUGENDER .... Being all genders in one's culture that one can be simultaneously or separately.

CONTIGENDER .... Flowing through space and time in a state of constant change, might be connected to space, time.

COOLCOLOREN .... Connected to cool colors.

COPGENDER .... A gender where one police's themselves internally.

CORNUCOPIAN .... Like mixing seasonal based genders over time.

CORRUBAONIC .... Connected to corruptions in video games.

CORUGENDER .... Changing during and around flashbacks due to one's mental disorder.

COSMICCORIC .... Like a cosmic entity, one with the universe when meditating.

COSMICGENDER .... So vast and complex its only processable incrementally.

COSTCOGENDER .... Connected to Costco Wholesale Corporation.

COTTAGECORIC .... Connected to romanticized imagery of agricultural life, harmony with nature, farms, animals, plants.

COTTONCANDYFLUID .... Fluid between Candyic genders.

COUNTRYGENDER .... Fluid, connected to living in countrysides.

COWBOYCORIC .... Connected to cowboys, Wild West culture.

COWGENDER (see Bullgender)

COYOTEGENDER .... Connected to coyotes, nature.

CRAYONCORIC .... Connected to crayons.

CRIMINOGENDER .... Unpredictable, unreliable, irrational acting.

CRIMSONGENDER .... Connected to the Crimson Forest biome in video game Minecraft, might be humid, like tropical climates, intense, aggressive.

CRISTALSOLUM .... Dark, connected to gems, rocks, color black, inner beauty.

CROSSIGEN .... Connected to video game Animal Crossing: New Horizons, might like peaceful island-experiences.

CROWCORIC .... Connected to crows.

CRYOSIC .... Cold, cryptic, stong connection to cryogenic freezing, might feel locked away, preserved, distant, nearly dead, trapped, might start to die but death is frozen incomplete.

CRYPTIDCORIC .... Connected to cryptozoology.

CRYPTOMANIC .... Rapid, frequent, hidden.

CRYSTALCORIC (Gendercrystal) .... Connected to crystals.

CRYSTALFORESTGENDER .... Connected to crystals, forests, magic.

CRYSTALLUMIAN .... Partially masculine, connected to crystals, ice, winter.

CUBEBOY ♂ .... Masculine variation of Cubegender.

CUBEGENDER .... Like a cube. {Cubeboy, Cubegirl, Cubenonbinary}

CUBEGIRL ♀ .... Feminine variation of Cubegender.

CUBENONBINARY

CUDDLEGENDER .... Soft, childlike, love, secure, like stuffed toys, nightlights, teddy bears.

CULTUBINARY ♂♀ .... Similar to male or female but gender identity is exclusive to one's culture or cultures.

CULTUHOARDER .... Hoarding genders exclusive to one's race, culture, ethnicity.

CUMULOGENDER (Dustbunnygender, Magnetgender) .... A gender that collects labels of itself.

CUPIDCORIC .... Connected to fictional creature Cupid.

CURAGENDER .... Connected to one's caregiver, or might be a caregiver, might change gender when reacting with a caregiver or one cared for.

CURATINEM .... A gender once ripped away now slowly being pieced together due to child abuse or neglect.

CUSTOFENEF .... Connected to video game Five Night At Freddy's Ultimate Custom Night, might only be felt when playing game.

CUTEGENDER (Gendercute; see Bellagender)

CYASOLUM .... Connected to ice, winter, moons, snow, angels, color cyan.

CYBER-ASTRAL .... Feeling made of stars, galaxies, celestial bodies, celestial energy, might feel like a supercomputer with self-modifying code.

CYBERGENDER (Gendertech, Pantechnicum, Techcoric, Technogender) .... Connected to technology.

CYBERGENDERPUNK .... Connected to by being cyberpunk or cyberpunk culture.

DADCORIC .... Connected to fathers, fathering.

DAEIX .... Demonic, hellish.

DAINGENDER (Delicagender, Elegender, Ethegender, Ethereagender) .... ethereal, delicate, elegant, unable to be understood and explained by either one's self or others.

DANGANIC (Danganronpagender) .... Connected to video games by Danganronpa.

DANGANRONPAGENDER (see Danganic)

DANGOGENDER .... Three genders skewered together but not mixed.

DARKANIAN .... Connected to darkness, night, winter, lanterns, cold wind.

DARKCOLOREN .... Connected to dark colors.

DARKGENDER .... Connected to dark colors or absence of color, or feeling like an absence of dark color.

DARKSMOKEUTIN .... Thick, smoky, smokes out other genders removing them.

DARKWEBGENDER .... Sinister, secret, usually illicit in nature.

DEATHDEITAEIC .... Feeling like a diety of death or embodiment of death, might be due to dissociative disorder.

DECEPTERIC .... Cutesy and innocent appearance with hidden devilish vibes.

DECORAGENDER .... Connected to bright colors, accessories, candy, Decora Kei fashion style.

DECREDOGENDER .... Connected to trauma from gaslighting making one constantly question its existence.

DEEPWEBGENDER .... Hidden, somewhat mysterious, usually harmless.

DEGENDER .... Connected to exhaustion or stress with its intensity dependent on level of stress or exhaustion.

DELICAGENDER (Elegender, Ethegender, Ethereagender; see Daingender)

DELICIAGENDER .... Multiple genders simultaneously but preferring one that fits better.

DELIFENAF .... Connected to video game Five Nights At Freddy's: Special Delivery, might only be felt when playing game.

DELUSOBOY♂ .... Masculine variation of Delusogender.

DELUSOGENDER .... Connected by one's delusions. {Delusoboy, Delusogirl}

DELUSOGIRL ♀ .... Feminine variation of Delusogender.

DEMIAECOR .... Partially feeling like water.

DEMIAGENDER (Demigender) .... Partially defined, partially undefined. {Demiboy, Demifemale, Demifemme, Demigal, Demigirl, Demiguy, Demigyne, Demiman, Demimasculine, Deminonbinary, Demiwoman}

DEMIBINARITY .... Partially binary, partially other.

DEMIBOY (Demiguy, Demiman, Demimasculine) ♂ .... Masculine variation of Demiagender.

DEMICAT (Demicatgender) .... Partially connected to cats, might be nonbinary.

DEMICATGENDER (see Demicat)

DEMICISGENDER .... Partially assigned gender at birth, partially other.

DEMIFAE .... Partially static, partially fluid between non-masculine genders.

DEMIFAON ♀ .... Feminine variation of Demifen.

DEMIFAONEN ♀ .... Feminine variation of Demfenen.

DEMIFELIBOY (Demifelimasc) ♂ .... Masculine variation of Demifeligender.

DEMIFELIFEM (Demifeligirl) ♀.......... Feminine variation of Demifeligender.

DEMIFELIGENDER (Demifelisgender) .... Partially connected to small cats {Demifeliboy, Demifelifem, Demifeligirl, Demifelimasc}

DEMIFELISGENDER (see Demifeligender)

DEMIFELIGIRL (see Demifelifem) ♀

DEMIFELIMASC (see Demifeliboy) ♂

DEMIFEMALE (Demifemme, Demigal, Demigirl, Demigyne, Demiwoman) ♀ .... Feminine variation of Demiagender.

DEMIFEMME (Demigal, Demigirl, Demigyne, Demiwoman; see Demifemale) ♀

DEMIFEN .... Partially unidentified static, partially fluid. {Demifaon, Demifeor, Demisylph}

DEMFENEN .... Partially undefined static, partially fluid never fully male or female. {Demifaonen, Demifeoren, Demisylphen}

DEMIDENFEMIA (Denfemia) ♀ .... Female but not being a woman.

DEMIFEOR ♂ .... Masculine variation of Demifen.

DEMIFEOREN ♂ .... Masculine variation of Demfenen.

DEMIFLIT .... Like a half full cup of water, might change due to emotions.

DEMIFLUID (Demiflux) .... Partially static, partially fluid.

DEMIFLUX (see Demifluid)

DEMIGAL (Demifemme, Demigirl, Demigyne, Demiwoman; see Demifemale) ♀

DEMIGENDER (see Demiagender)

DEMIGIRL (Demifemme, Demigal, Demigyne, Demiwoman; see Demifemale) ♀

DEMIGUY (Demiman, Demimasculine; see Demiboy) ♂

DEMIGYNE (Demifemme, Demigal, Demigirl, Demiwoman; see Demifemale) ♀

DEMIMAN (Demiguy, Demimasculine; see Demiboy) ♂

DEMIMASCULINE (Demiguy, Demiman; see Demiboy) ♂

DEMINONBINARY .... Nonbinary variation of Demiagender.

DEMIPANTHAGENDER .... Partially connected to big cats.

DEMIPUP .... Partially connected to dogs, might be nonbinary.

DEMI-SMOKE (Demi-Vapor) .... Transcendental, spiritual, preventing other genders from being seen and understood, might be due to dark emotions.

DEMISYLPH .... Nonbinary variation of Demifen.

DEMISYLPHEN .... Nonbinary variation of Demfenen.

DEMI-VAPOR (see Demi-Smoke)

DEMIWILDGENDER .... Partially connected to Wildgender.

DEMIWOMAN (Demifemme, Demigal, Demigirl, Demigyne; see Demifemale) ♀

DEMONCORIC .... Connected to demons, fallen angels, related creatures.

DEMONGENDER (Demonicgender) .... Connected to anything demonic, including fiction, real, mythological.

DEMONICGENDER (see Demongender)

DENFEMIA (see Demidenfemia) ♀

DENGENDER .... Like a cave, rocky, dark.

DENVIR ♂ .... Male but not being a man.

DERKAZGENDER .... Feeling parts of one's gender are hidden or concealed in darkness.

DEUSOLUM .... Connected to Greek gods, color green, stars, nature.

DEUXSOLUM .... Connected to lust, color pink, flower crowns, angels, demons.

DIBELLIC .... Tries being beautiful to others, other worldy energy.

DICEMBRIAN .... Cold, frosty, constantly cycled around other genders, might be connected to snow, end of the year, frozen rain.

DICTITOGENDER .... A gender feeling reintegrated into one's self many times.

DIGGENDER .... A gender getting deeper and deeper as one gets older.

DIRTCORIC .... Connected to dirt.

DISCORDIAN .... Chaotic, hard to comprehend and explain, might be one gender or multiple genders.

DISCORIC .... Connected to Disco music and culture.

DIVIGENDER .... Feeling one's gender is divided up, might be due to dissociative disorder, other mental disorder.

DIVISIGENDER .... A gender not male and female due to being intersex.

DJENDER .... Harsh, jagged.

DOGCORIC (Puppycoric) .... Connected to dogs.

DOGENDER (Doggender) .... Strong connection to dogs due to being autistic.

DOGGENDER (see Dogender)

DOLCHECHAUFBOY ♂ .... Masculine variation of Dolchechaufgender.

DOLCHECHAUFGENDER .... Soft, warm. like candlelight. {Dolchechaufboy, Dolchechaufgirl}

DOLCHECHAUFGIRL ♀ .... Feminine variation of Dolchechaufgender.

DOLLCORIC (Dollyic) .... Connected to dolls, figurines.

DOLLCORIC (see Dollcoric)

DOMGENDER (Genderbox) .... More than one gender with one more dominant than the others.

DOMINONIAN .... A gender that collapses to be followed by other genders collapsing.

DRACHEGENUS .... Deep lifelong connections to dragons. {Drachenboy, Drachenfeminine, Drachenfemme, Drachengirl, Drachenmasc}

DRACHENBOY (Drachenmasc) ♂ .... Masculine variation of Drachengenus.

DRACHENMASC (see Drachenboy) ♂

DRACHENFEMININE (Drachenfemme, Drachengirl) ♀ .... Feminine variation of Drachengenus.

DRACHENFEMME (Drachengirl; see Drachenfeminine) ♀

DRACHENGIRL (Drachenfemme; see Drachenfeminine) ♀

DRACOBOY ♂ .... Masculine variation of Dracogender.

DRACOGENDER .... Like a dragon, winged, large. {Dracoboy, Femdracogender}

DRACONSTOSIC .... Neutral, connected to dragons, might feel safe and secure like the dragon is a protective guardian.

DRAGONGENDER .... Connected to dragons.

DRAGONNESOLUM .... Connected to lizards, witchcraft, color orange, nonconformity.

DRAKEFLUID .... Fluctuating gender not describable in few terms so one hoards gender terms.

DREADIC .... Connected to character Dreadbear of video game Five Nights At Freddy's, might feel put together, evil, large, malicious, mechanical.

DREAMCORIC .... Connected to dreams.

DROPLEN .... Like a single drop of water.

DRUNKOREXGENDER .... Connected to one's alcohol abuse with bulimia or anorexia.

DRYAGENDER .... Like an empty forest.

DSgender .... Connected to Nintendo DS video games or system.

DS-Wiigender .... Connected to DS and Wii era of Nintendo video game system.

DUBIUCINE .... Gender Apathetic partially or in flux.

DULCIGENDER .... Connected to stereotypically feminine things such as buns, frills, color pink, cute things.

DULLGENDER .... Dull but still noticeable.

DUNWINE .... Connected to old crumbling houses, gloomy abandoned places.

DUOGENDER .... Identifying as binary or combination due to being intersex.

DURAGENDER .... Multi-Gender where one gender is more identifiable, long-lasting, prominent.

DUSTBUNNYGENDER (Magnetgender; see Cumulogender)

DUSTFLUID .... Fluid, dusty, might feel worn away one day and intact another.

DVDSCREENSAVERGENDER .... Like floating around in a void.

DYSPHORIAGENDER .... Connected to one's gender dysphoria, fluctuates or disappears at times.

EARTHGENDER .... Mysterious, connected to the earth, nature, like a deity involved with the earth who has mood swings, changing identities.

EARTH PONY (Pegasus, Unicorn; see Ponygender)

EDUCORIC (Schoolcoric) .... Connected to education, schooling.

EFEMIGENDER (Afeminigender, Afeminogender, Efeminigender, Effeminigender, Effeminogender, Ginandrigender, Ginandrogender, Gynandrigender, Gynandrogender; see Afemigender) ♂♀

EFEMINIGENDER (Afeminigender, Afeminogender, Efemigender, Effeminigender, Effeminogender, Ginandrigender, Ginandrogender, Gynandrigender, Gynandrogender; see Afemigender) ♂♀

EFFEMINIGENDER Afeminigender, Afeminogender, Efemigender, Efeminigender, Effeminogender, Ginandrigender, Ginandrogender, Gynandrigender, Gynandrogender; see Afemigender) ♂♀

EFFEMINOGENDER (Afeminigender, Afeminogender, Efemigender, Efeminigender, Effeminigender, Ginandrigender, Ginandrogender, Gynandrigender, Gynandrogender; see Afemigender) ♂♀

EGOGENDER (Namegender; see Charagender)

ELDRIGENDER .... Dark, nebulous, ultimately unknowable.

ELEGENDER (Delicagender, Ethegender, Ethereagender; see Daingender)

ELEPHANILLIC .... Nervous, overwhelming, immense, slow-moving, might be due to trauma.

ELLIPSOIDIC .... Multi-Gender with one taking the most attention leaving all others in the dark somewhat perceivable.

EMBERDEINE .... Connected to embers, small fires, warm objects, soft blankets, cold winter nights.

EMBERFLUID .... Like a flame flaring up and disappearing.

EMERALDGENDER .... Neutral, nonbinary, fluid, connected to emeralds.

EMETOGENDER .... Experiencing different genders when vomiting.

EMOCATGENDER .... Catgender, Emocoric.

EMOCORIC .... Connected to Emo music and culture.

EMOJIGENDER .... Best described by emojis.

EMOTICONGENDER .... Best described by emoticons.

ENBIE (Gender Nonconforming, Genderqueer, Gender Variant, Nonbinary, Third Gender, X-Gender; see Cogender)

ENDERGENDER .... Connected to Endermen characters of video game Minecraft, might have a difficult relationship with gender.

ENERGENDER .... Like a ball of energy via moving rapidly, not being able to be pinned down. {Energender Boy, Energender Girl}

ENERGENDER BOY ♂ .... Masculine variation of Energender.

ENERGENDER GIRL ♀ .... Feminine variation of Energender.

ENIGENDER (Visigender, Visuogender) .... Fluid, not accurately describable with spoken or written language, but can be described via audio, pictures, video or other means, might appear differently to different people.

ENNARDGENDER .... Connected to character Ennard of video game Five Nights at Freddy's: Sister Location, might be dark, malicious, twisted, manipulative, mechanical, desperate for freedom, wishing to hide inside of another gender.

EONIABAONIC .... A gender going on forever, or might be one looks forever to find it.

EPICENE (Gender Neutral) .... Gender neutral or Agender, or having no gender characteristics.

EQUIBINARY .... Experiencing binary genders perfectly equally.

ERBAGENDER .... Animalistic, otherworldly, connected to plants.

ERISIAN (Merjuparian) ♂ .... Fluid between Juparian and Mercurian.

ERROFLUID .... Fluid, connected to one's psychotic symptoms.

ERRORICINE .... Cold, chaotic, brutal, like a computer glitch.

ESCAPIGENDER .... Connected to one's maladaptive daydreaming, might be Agender during dreams, might have a feeling of being gone.

ESENCEAUX .... A gender creating a transcendental vague experience from the abstraction of one's gender in its rudimentary form, might have a Gnostic sense of self.

ESMOGENDER .... Causing one to feel certain emotions, or only felt when experiencing certain emotions.

ESPIGENDER .... Connected to spirit beings or entities existing on an extra-dimensional plane.

ETHALE ♀ .... Connected to womanhood but existing as a separate gender.

ETHEGENDER (Delicagender, Elegender, Ethereagender; see Daingender)

ETHEREAGENDER (Delicagender, Elegender, Ethegender; see Daingender)

ETHEREALGENDER .... Vague, formless, connected soft satin fabric, night's breeze, floating in the void of space, weightless in water, might be connected to multiple genders, music.

ETORGENDER .... A gender present all or majority of the time becoming stronger with age regression.

EUCLIGENDER .... Unpredictable and misunderstood to point of being hard to describe.

EUNUCH ♂ .... Assigned male at birth but with some or all male genitals removed deliberately or without consent.

EVERYBODYVOTESCHANNELGENDER .... Connected to Everybody Votes Channel from Wii.

EVERYGENDER .... Many genders where its easier to lump them all together, might relate to all genders.

EVILCORIC .... Connected to evil.

EXANGUISIAN .... Pale or bloodless like having lost all energy, barely existing.

EXEMGENDER .... Animalistic, otherworldly.

EXGENDER .... A gender with an outright refusal to accept or identify in, on, around gender spectrums.

EXISTGENDER .... A gender simply existing.

EXISTIGENDER (see Cogitogender)

EXOBINARY (Midbinary) .... Mixing both binary genders without being fully binary.

EXPLORCANUM .... Deep, profound, fluid with mystical and arcane feelings effecting one deeply.

EXTERBINARY (Offbinary; see Abinary)

FABRICGENDER (Parougender) .... Connected to one's presentation or clothing.

FACSIMILIQUE .... Feeling like a copy of another gender, might serve a purpose.

FAEGENDER .... Changing with seasons, equinoxes, moon phases.

FAESARI ♀ .... A gender most comfortable within gender neutral spectrum but feeling strong attachments to femininity.

FEATHEIC .... Like feathers scattered on the ground, might hoard genders.

FAICHEIAN .... Connected to color green.

FAIRYCORIC .... Connected to fae.

FAIRYLICHT .... Connected to fairy lights, gives off soft vibes, can light other genders.

FAIRYPUPGENDER .... Connected to fairies, puppies.

FANDOMGENDER .... Connected to a fan scene of something in popular culture.

FANDOMPAGEGENDER .... Connected to a certain part of fandom.com website.

FANDOMWIKIGENDER (Genderfandom) .... Connected to fandom.com website.

FARMCORIC .... Connected to farms, farming.

FASCIFLUX .... Fluctuating based on one's special interests due to being autistic.

FATUGENDER .... Having a useless gender.

FATUM .... Connected to death, Halloween, decorations, emptiness, being missing.

FAUNAGENDER (see Animalcoric)

FAVILLAEGENDER .... Like burning embers, war, charred, barely existing.

FAVILLARIC (Nokoribic) .... Soft, gentle, burning with passion.

FEATHERIPIM .... A gender floating like feathers coming to rest.

FELINEGENDER (Speciesgender) .... Connected to specific species of cat.

FELOIDGENDER .... Partially feeling like a cat.

FELSICFLUX .... Changes very gradually or rarely, might have intense sudden change.

FEMAGENUS CHRISTIAN ♀ .... Christian, nonbinary, connected to femininity.

FEMALE .... Social construct related to femininity

FEMALE-TO-MALE (FTM) ♂♀ .... Assigned female at birth but now male.

FEMALE-TO-NEUTER TRANSEXUAL (FTN) ♀ .... Female-to-neuter transsexual.

FEMDRACOGENDER ♀ .... Feminine variation of Dracogender.

FEMFLUID ♀ .... Fluctuating feelings limited to feminine genders.

FEMFLUIDFLUX ♀ .... Feminine variation of Fluidflux.

FEMGENDER ♀ .... Feminine in nature.

FEMINAFIDEM ♀ .... Christian, Trans.

FEMME ♀ .... Leaning towards feminine in some way.

FEM-TENEBRAIC ♀ .... Feminine variation of Tenebraic.

FENEFCUATRO .... Connected to fourth Five Nights At Freddy's video game, might only be felt when playing game.

FENAFDOS .... Connected to second Five Nights At Freddy's video game, might only be felt when playing game.

FENEFNOVELO .... Connected to Five Night At Freddy's novels, might only be felt when playing game.

FENAFSEIS .... Connected to video game Freddy Fazbear's Pizzeria Simulator, might only be felt when playing game.

FENAFSIETE .... Connected to video game Five Nights At Freddy's: Help Wanted, might only be felt when playing game.

FENAFTRES .... Connected to third Five Nights At Freddy's video game, might only be felt when playing game.

FENAFUNO .... Connected to first Five Nights At Freddy's video game, might only be felt when playing game.

FENCEGENDER .... Having to climb over one gender to reach another.

FENGENDER .... Like the wind, playful, fickle, spread out.

FERAGENDER .... Connected to wild animals, nature, might be detached from social norms.

FERRGENDER .... Animalistic, otherworldly, connected to steel.

FERVEOGENDER .... Turbulant, warm, frantic, burnt, might surge over time.

FEUTEGENDER .... Being deceptively dark, evil outside but inside being sweet, cute, innocent.

FICTIGENDER .... Connected to works of fiction, fictional characters, events, locations.

FIDEMGENDRE .... Christian, nonbinary.

FIELDCORIC .... Connected to fields.

FIREFOXGENDER .... Simple, minimalistic.

FIREGENDER BOY ♂ .... Masculine variation of Firegender.

FIREGENDER .... Constant state of flux, connected to passion, strength, fire, might be destructive, deadly when misused. {Firegender Boy, Firegender Girl}

FIREGENDER GIRL ♀ .... Feminine variation of Firegender.

FISSGENDER .... Feeling split between more than one gender with all separate and not overlapping.

FLAGGENDER .... Wavy, free, colorful, floaty like a flag.

FLAMMAENINE .... Connected to fire, hellish flames, scorching warmth.

FLASHGENDER .... Quick, bright, coming and going in large fluxes.

FLAVOSOLUM .... Connected to sunshine, space, stars, happiness, color yellow.

FLEXANATIS .... Connected to rubber ducks, might be buoyant, childish, color yellow.

FLITBOY ♂ .... Masculine variation of Flitzan.

FLITGIRL ♀ .... Feminine variation of Flitzan.

FLITZAN .... Static, like a full cup of water. {Flitboy, Flitgirl, Flitzenby}

FLITZENBY .... Nonbinary variation of Flitzan.

FLIUX (Fluix, Fluidflux, Fluxfluid, Genderfliux, Genderfluix) .... Fluid between two or more genders fluctuating in intensity over time. {Femfluidflux, Mascfluidflux}

FLORAGENDER .... Connected to plants, flowers.

FLOWERCORE (Flowercoric) .... Connected to flowers, or like a flower.

FLOWERCORIC (see Flowercore)

FLUFFYBOY ♂ .... Masculine variation of Fluffygender.

FLUFFYGENDER (Genderfluffy) .... Connected to soft textures, objects. {Fluffyboy, Fluffygirl}

FLUFFYGIRL ♀ .... Feminine variation of Fluffygender.

FLUIX (Fluidflux, Fluxfluid, Genderfliux, Genderfluix; see Fliux)

FLUIDFLUX (Fluix, Fluxfluid, Genderfliux, Genderfluix; see Fliux)

FLUOROGENDER .... Connected to fluorescent colors, fluorescence.

FLUXFLUID (Fluix, Fluidflux, Genderfliux, Genderfluix; see Fliux)

FLUXODUMGENDER .... Fluid, frequent change to avoid distress, might be due to trauma.

FNAFgender .... Fluid, connected to video games Five Nights At Freddy's.

FOGGENDER (Genderfog, Gendervague, Nebbiagender) .... Not knowing or understanding one's gender due to fatigue or dissociation. {Nebbiaboy, Nebbiagirl}

FOODCORIC (Foodgender, Gastrongender, Nutriencegender) .... Connected to food, might be connected to drink.

FOODGENDER (Gastrongender, Nutriencegender; see Foodcoric)

FORASGENUS .... Christian, anonbinary

FORESTCORE (Forestcoric) .... Connected to forests.

FORESTCORIC (see Forestcoric)

FORESTGENDER .... Connected to nature, forests as gender itself.

FORTGENDER .... Built like a fort with hard outer walls and vulnerable town inside.

FORTNITEGENDER .... Connected to video game Fortnite.

FOXCORIC .... Connected to foxes.

FRACTALGENDER .... Composed of many different patterns or components.

FREDDLIC .... Connected to character the Freddles of video game Five Nights At Freddy's, might be watchful, hidden, malicious, sometimes shymechanical.

FREDIC .... Connected to the character Freddy of video game Five Nights At Freddy's, might be sneaky, dangerous, watchful, feeling mechanical.

FREDGENDER .... Connected to characters of video games Five Nights At Freddy's.

FREMULTI .... Connected to multiple Fredgenders of video game Five Nights At Freddy's simultaneously or separate.

FRIENDCORIC .... Connected to friendship, might be influenced by one's friends.

FROGGENDER .... Connected to frogs.

FTM (see FEMALE-TO-MALE) ♂♀

FTN (see FEMALE-TO-NEUTER TRANSEXUAL) ♀

FUCHSIAC .... Connected to Fuchsias and their colors.

FUCHSIANIX .... Connected to pillows, sunsets, sunrises, flamingos, shrimp, colors pink and fuchsia.

FULGENDER .... Animalistic, otherworldly, connected to electricity.

FUNCORIC .... Connected to fun things, activities.

FUNTIC (see Bonic)

FUTURAEGENDER .... Lacking of gender in the present time but feeling one might gain a gender in the future.

FUTUREFUNKIC .... Connected to vaporwave music off-shoot future funk and related culture.

FUZZGENDER .... Knowing one is a certain gender but can't explain why.

FYRIAN .... Slightly Pangender, connected to fire, camping, winter, fireplaces, candles, wind.

GALAGIC .... Orderly, logical, calm, underlying feeling of power, other worldly energy.

GALAXIEGENDER .... Vast, mysterious, like a galaxy, or might be connected to space.

GAMECORIC (Gamegender) .... Connected to all types of games, gaming.

GAMEGENDER (see Gamecoric)

GARDENCORIC .... Connected to gardens, gardening.

GASTRONGENDER (Foodgender, Nutriencegender; see Foodcoric)

GATSGENDER ♂♀ .... Associated with definition of masculinity or femininity of the 1920's flapper culture versus pre-2000 interpretations.

GAYGENDER (Vinciangender; see Achilleangender) ♂

GELSOLUM .... Bright, connected to ice, foxes, color blue, oceans.

GEMIGENDER .... Two opposite genders working together fluidly.

GENDERABYSSALIS .... Dark, deep, abyssal.

GENDER AGNOSTIC .... A gender with no preference for any gender, might opt out of gender systems.

GENDERALBUM .... Foggy, thin, connected to snow, cold weather, color white.

GENDERAMBURO .... Slightly scorched or burnt.

GENDERANXIOUS .... Undefined gender because finding a gender label or having a gender triggers anxiety.

GENDER APATHETIC .... A gender not identifying with, nor having an opinion, nor caring about any particular gender, might accept one's assigned gender at birth or being nonbinary.

GENDERAPOTHECA .... Feeling small compared to other genders, might be Multi-Gender.

GENDERATRAM (Genderpiceum) .... Somewhat dark and vague, connected to night, winter, color black, might be invisible or nearly invisible being thin like glass.

GENDERATROPURPUREUM .... Dark, connected to spring nights, flowers after rain, over-flowing rivers, rain, might be calming like gentle rainfall.

GENDERATRUM .... Shrouded in darkness, feeling gloomy, unwelcoming, isolated.

GENDERAZURINUM .... Rainy, connected to winter, frost, ice, blizzards, gentle snowfall.

GENDERBI .... Connected to one's bisexuality.

GENDERBLANK .... Only describable as a blank space as when the gender is called into question all that comes to mind is a blank space.

GENDERBLAVUM .... Rainy, cool, connected to winter, dying flowers, frozen lakes, snow covered trees, freezing cold weather, color blue.

GENDERBOREALISSIMUS .... Light, colorful, connected to northerly directions, rain, snowfall, glaciers.

GENDERBOX (see Domgender)

GENDERBRUISED (see Bruisegender)

GENDERCAERULEUM .... Connected to rain, winter, snow, frozen lakes, cold nights, might be calming like gentle snow fall.

GENDERCALEFECERE .... Feeling warm, quickly cools.

GENDERCANDELIA .... Bright, scented, colorful, connected to candles, fire.

GENDERCANDIDUM .... Airy, clear, connected to candles, light, evenings, color white.

GENDERCANUM .... White, frothy, connected to fireplaces, cold weather, winter, color white.

GENDERCEREUM .... Fiery, clear, connected to candles, wax, autumn, colors white, yellow.

GENDERCHALOOUIN (Chaloouinfluix; see Chaloouinfluid)

GENDERCIMITERIUM .... Trapped, feeling buried under other genders, connected to graveyards.

GENDERCINEREUM .... Grey, airy, connected to candles, fire, ash, fireplaces

GENDERCLOCK .... Connected with time, clocks, might be connected to time travel and history.

GENDERCOLORIUS .... Colorful, connected to rainbows, summer.

GENDERCROW .... Hoarding cold, sharp, dark, protective, dangerous genders.

GENDERCRYSTAL (see Crystalcoric)

GENDERCUTE (Cutegender, Gendercute; see Bellagender)

GENDERDISTURBED .... A gender one doesn't try to define as it makes one feel repulsed, frightened, anxious, disturbed by it.

GENDERDOE (Genderfae, Genderthil) .... Fluid between multiple non-masculine genders.

GENDEREBEREUM .... White, large, connected to ivory, wind, winter, might be warm.

GENDERESSIMAL .... A gender being infinitesimal.

GENDERFAE (Genderthil, see Genderdoe)

GENDERFAER .... Fluid between multiple genders not including binary male.

GENDERFANDOM (see Fandomwikigender)

GENDERFAUN (Gendermars) .... Fluid between multiple non-feminine genders.

GENDERFAUNET .... Fluid between multiple genders not including binary female.

GENDERFAKE .... Feeling one's gender is hallucinations or delusions, might be due to mental disorders.

GENDERFAON (Genderfen, Genderfeor, Gendersylph) .... Exclusively fluid between Aliagenders and other genders not identifying on binary spectrum, might change randomly, fluctuate intensities.

GENDERFAONEN (Genderfenen, Genderfeoren, Gendersylphen) .... Exclusively fluid between Aliagenders, masculine and feminine genders not identifying on binary spectrum, might change randomly, fluctuate intensities.

GENDERFAONER (Genderfener, Genderfeorer, Gendersylpher) ♂ .... Exclusively fluid between Aliagenders and masculine genders identifying as nonbinary or on masculine spectrum, might change randomly, fluctuate intensities.

GENDERFAONET (Genderfenet, Genderfeoret, Gendersylphet) ♀ .... Exclusively fluid between Aliagenders and feminine genders identifying as nonbinary or on feminine spectrum, might change randomly, fluctuate intensities.

GENDERFEN (Genderfeor, Gendersylph; see Genderfaon)

GENDERFENEN (Genderfeoren, Gendersylphen; see Genderfaonen)

GENDERFENER (Genderfeorer, Gendersylpher; see Genderfaoner) ♂

GENDERFENET (Genderfeoret, Gendersylphet; see Genderfaonet) ♀

GENDERFEOR (Genderfen, Gendersylph; see Genderfaon)

GENDERFEOREN (Genderfenen, Gendersylphen; see Genderfaonen)

GENDERFEORER (Genderfener, Gendersylpher; see Genderfaoner) ♂

GENDERFEORET (Genderfenet, Gendersylphet; see Genderfaonet) ♀

GENDERFLIUX (Fluix, Fluidflux, Fluxfluid, Genderfluix; see Fliux)

GENDERFLOR (Gendervae) .... Fluid between multiple genders not including binary female and male.

GENDERFLOW (see Aquarigender)

GENDERFLUFF .... FLUFFYGENDER (Genderfluffy) .... Connected to soft textures, objects, warm, light hearted.

GENDERFLUFFY (see Fluffygender)

GENDERFLUIX (Fluix, Fluidflux, Fluxfluid, Genderfliux; see Fliux)

GENDERFLUX .... Feeling one's gender fluctuating in intensity, fluid between Pangender and Agender.

GENDERFOG (Gendervague, Nebbiagender; see Foggender)

GENDERFONCEE ♀ .... Dark, secluded.

GENDERFORCED .... Agender, experiencing a gender due to trauma from abuse.

GENDERFREE (Genderless, Non-Gendered; see Agender)

GENDERFUMOSUS .... Like a plume of smoke, appears and floats up into other genders, eventually dissolves.

GENDERFUZZ (see Genderfuzz)

GENDERGALBINUM (Gendergalbum) .... Flowery, warm, connected to blooming flowers, spring, sun, meadows, ponds, might be like wheat in a field moving with the wind.

GENDERGALBUM (see Gendergalbinum)

GENDERGAY .... With a gay orientation regardless of gender.

GENDERGELID .... Connected to ice, bitter cold weather.

GENDERGLITCHED .... A gender only half there.

GENDERGOTHICA .... Gothic, connected to traditional Gothic culture.

GENDERGRISEUM .... Grey, vague, connected to smoke from a chimney, cabins, winter, might be smokey, emotionally indifferent.

GENDERGRUNGE .... Connected to Grunge music and culture.

GENDERHAUK .... Hoarding Orientationgenders.

GENDERHEBES .... Boring, dull, translucent.

GENDERHOARDER .... Hoarder of genders.

GENDERHOLLOW .... A gender feeling present but being empty or hollow.

GENDERHOODIE .... Surrounded by warmth, comfort.

GENDERHOUSE .... Neutral, comfortable.

GENDERIANTHEUM .... Dark, rainy, connected to autumn weather, flowers in the rain, flowing rivers, might be calming like gentle rainfall.

GENDERILARGI .... Like a comfortable night on a beach.

GENDERINIMICUS (Kynigender) .... Connected to one's anxiety disorder causing anxiousness or depression or stress, might cause one to restart the investigation.

GENDERJUICE .... A fluid gender being bright and tangy when changing.

GENDERKRIEG .... Multiple genders harshly contradicting each another, might be connected to personality disorders.

GENDERLESS (Genderfree, Non-Gendered; see Agender)

GENDERLAINO .... Comfortable, misty, like rain falling, windy forests.

GENDERLIBERA .... Flamboyant, connected to pianos.

GENDERLIVIDUM .... Rainy, connected to evenings, bugs, lakes, rain, forests, might be like gentle rainfall.

GENDERMARMOREUM .... Flamboyant, fancy, connected to marble, mountains, winter, color white.

GENDERMARS (see Genderfaun)

GENDERMELT .... Soft, feeling melted but not fully fluid.

GENDERMETUS .... Dark, beautiful.

GENDERMISSILIS .... Like was shot through the atmosphere.

GENDERMOLLIS .... Intimidating looking but actually being gentle, soft.

GENDERMORTES (Gendernekros) .... A gender fading into death.

GENDERMORTUSS .... Feeling dead, barely clinging to life.

GENDERMUTE .... A gender making itself known only in safe environments where one can speak openly.

GENDERNEKROS (see Gendermortes)

GENDER NEUTRAL (see Epicene)

GENDERNIER .... Very dark and vague, connected to night, summer, color black, might be invisible or nearly invisible being thin like glass.

GENDERNIMIUS .... Connected to one's hyperactivity, might be due to one's AHCD.

GENDERNIVEUM .... White, snowy, connected to candles, winter weather, frost.

Gendernoia .... Connected to one's paranoia.

GENDER NONCONFORMING (Enbie, Genderqueer, Gender Variant, Nonbinary, Third Gender, X-Gender; see Cogender)

GENDEROCCIDENTALISSIMUS .... Airy, colorful, connected to westerly directions, salt, canyons, forests, deserts, might be free-spirited, might be deeply connected to the earth.

GENDEROPAQUE .... Not transparent.

GENDERORIENTALISSIMUS .... Bright, colorful, connected to easterly directions, sunrise, mountains, rivers.

GENDERPACATUS .... Pacified, peaceful, changing into a smaller gender when interrupted.

GENDERPASTEL .... Pastel, gentle, soft, quiet.

GENDERPAX .... Bright, airy, peaceful.

GENDERPICEUM (see Genderatram)

GENDERPILE .... Multiple genders in a disorganized stack.

GENDERPINK (Pinkcore, Pinkgender) .... Connected to color pink.

GENDERPLUMBEUM .... Grey, poisonous, connected to mountains, winter, smoke.

GENDERPLUSH .... Connected to teddy bears.

GENDERPULLUM .... Grey, small, connected to fog, smoke, winter.

GENDERPUNK .... A gender actively resisting gender norms.

GENDERPURPUREUM .... Bright, flowery, connected to flowers, spring showers, spring evenings.

GENDERPYRAMIS ♂ .... Tall, proud, might be connected to pyramids, deserts.

GENDERQUEER (Enbie, Gender Nonconforming, Gender Variant, Nonbinary, Third Gender, X-Gender; see Cogender)

GENDERRAVUM .... Grey, large, cloudy, connected to rain, glass, winter.

GENDERROSEUM .... Bright, flowery, connected to spring weather, flowers, flowing rivers, rain, color rose, might be calming like gentle rainfall.

GENDERSAPO .... Solid but fragile feeling.

GENDERSELKIE .... Fluid between multiple genders including Xenine.

GENDERSHIP .... Connected to boats, ships, might be connected to maritime things in general.

GENDERSINK .... A gender identity weighing one down towards trauma, might have losing sense of self, anxiety, depression.

GENDERSPLOOF .... Connected to blankets, poofy objects.

GENDERSTALGIA .... Connected to sunsets, nostalgia, might be connected to romance.

GENDERSTIM .... Wiggles, bounces happily.

GENDERSTITCH .... Consisting of pieces from other genders stitched together.

GENDERSYLPH (Genderfen, Genderfeor, Gendersylphen; see Genderfaon)

GENDERSYLPHEN (Genderfenen, Genderfeoren; see Genderfaonen)

GENDERSYLPHER (Genderfener, Genderfeorer; see Genderfaoner)

GENDERSYLPHET (Genderfenet, Gendersylphet; see Genderfaonet)

GENDERTECH (Pantechnicum, Techcoric, Technogender; see Cybergender)

GENDERTEXTUS .... A gender woven into other genders.

GENDERTHIL (Genderfae; see Genderdoe)

GENDERVAE (see Genderflor)

GENDERVAGUE (Genderfog, Nebbiagender; see Foggender)

GENDER VARIANT (Enbie, Gender Nonconforming, Genderqueer, Nonbinary, Third Gender, X-Gender; see Cogender)

GENDERVAST .... Fluid between Xenine and nonbinary.

GENDERVENETUM .... Rainy, connected to summer, flowers, lakes, might be like calming gentle rainfall.

GENDERVENERES .... Created by fluid movement of Veneresfluid.

GENDERVINDEMI .... Vintage feeling.

GENDERVIOLACEUM .... Bright, gentle, connected to autumn weather, flowers in a forest, flowing rivers, rain, color violet.

GENDERVOID (Void, Voidgender) .... Consisting of a void, might be Agender.

GENDERWAX .... A gender melting going from static to fluid and back.

GENDERWEIRD (Pomogender) .... A gender where no current labels apply.

GENDERWHAT .... A gender with confusion and apathy towards being either a fluid or stable gender.

GENDERWICK .... Fluid gender melting and disappearing.

GENDERWITCHED .... A gender where one is intrigued by the idea of a particular gender but not necessarily feeling it.

GENDERXEUCCIAN .... Connected to funny things, feels randomly created.

GENGENDER (see Allekeinegender)

GERSTLAUERGENDER .... Connected to Germany based amusement ride manufacturer Gerstlauer, might have multiple inversions, intense, nimble.

GHOSTGORIC .... Connected to ghosts.

GHOSTPUPGENDER .... Connected to dogs with ghostly qualities, might be connected to departed pet dogs, might be disconnected from people, feeling misunderstood, feeling unseen.

GILVUSFLUID .... Colorful, sunny, color yellow.

GIRLFLUX ♀ .... Feeling mostly or all female most of the time with fluctuating intensities of feminine gender identity.

GINANDRIGENDER (Afeminigender, Afeminogender, Efemigender, Efeminigender, Effeminigender, Effeminogender, Ginandrogender, Gynandrigender, Gynandrogender; see Afemigender) ♂♀

GINANDROGENDER (Afeminigender, Afeminogender, Efemigender, Efeminigender, Effeminigender, Effeminogender, Ginandrigender, Gynandrigender, Gynandrogender, see Afemigender) ♂♀

GIUGNETTUIAN .... Hot, sunny, connected to summer, beaches, sandy shores, tropical environments, more intense than Giugnuian gender.

GIUGNUIAN .... Hot, sunny, connected to summer, beaches, sandy shores, tropical environments.

GLACGENDER .... Animalistic, otherworldly, connected to ice.

GLACIESIAN ♂ .... Like ice.

GLASIAN .... Feeling thin and breakable like glass.

GLASSGENDER .... Very sensitive, fragile.

GLIMRAGENDER .... Faintly shining and wavering.

GLITRUM .... Glittery, nonbinary.

GLITTERCORIC (Glittergender) .... Connected to glitter.

GLITTERGENDER (see Glittercoric)

GLOENDER .... Fluidly moving from light to dark.

GLUCIC .... Changing with one's blood sugar levels, might be same gender changing or changing between genders.

GLUEGENDER .... Sticky, important feeling.

GOLDIC .... Connected to character Golden Freddy/Yellow Bear of video game Five Nights At Freddy's, might be broken, spastic, sporadic, mysterious, dangerous, mechanical.

GOOPGENDER .... Stretchy, bouncy.

GOREAEIC (Gorecoric) .... Connected to gore, death.

GORECORIC (see Goreaeic)

GOSSAGENDER .... So weak it is barely there, or feels fragile.

GOTHCORIC (Gothgender, Noirgender) .... Connected to goth culture or being goth, might be connected to gothic themed music.

GOTHGENDER (Noirgender, see Gothcoric)

GRANDELUSOGENDER .... Connected to delusions of grandeur.

GRANDESOLUM .... Soft, connected to strength, anger, claws, fangs.

GRANDMACORIC .... Connected to grandmothers.

GRAVLAEIX .... Connected to Earth, rocks.

GRAYGENDER .... Experiencing ambivalence about one's gender identity or expression, might not fully identify as exclusively binary.

GRAYSCALEN .... Connected to colors on gray scale.

GREENGENDER .... Connected to color green.

GREYGENDER .... Having weak gender identification.

GRISESOLUM .... Connected to rainy days, hot chocolate, moons, winter, color gray.

GUISGENDER .... Animalistic, otherworldly, connected to dragons.

GXRL ♀ .... Both feminine and no gender simultaneously or separate.

GYNANDRIGENDER (Afeminigender, Afeminogender, Efemigender, Efeminigender, Effeminigender, Effeminogender, Ginandrigender, Ginandrogender, Gynandrogender; see Afemigender) ♂♀

GYNANDROGENDER (Afeminigender, Afeminogender, Efemigender, Efeminigender, Effeminigender, Effeminogender, Ginandrigender, Ginandrogender, Gynandrigender; see Afemigender) ♂♀

GYNX ♀ .... Between female and Androgyne.

GYRAGENDER .... Multiple genders but understanding none of them.

GXNDERFLUIX (see Agenderfluix)

HADENGENDER .... A gender or genders feeling weaker when one is depressed.

HALCYON .... Bittersweet like remembering childhood.

HALLOWFLUID .... Fluid, connected to Halloween, autumn, winter based genders.

HALLOWGENDER (Lumnic) .... Silly, connected to Halloween.

HALLUCIGENDER .... Connected to hallucinations, delusions, might be due to mental disorders.

HARAGENDER .... Lolitagender, Partygender, Decoragender.

HARBORIC .... Connected to harbors, sea, fish, nautical things.

HARVESTMOONINE .... Connected to traditional annual harvest, harvest moon.

HATEGENDER (see Angegender)

HAZOMNIGENDER .... Hazy like a dream.

HEALGENDER .... Bringing lots of peace, clarity, security, creativity.

HEARTCORIC .... Connected to hearts, or feels like it beats like a heart.

HEARTIC .... A gender felt in one's heart but the gender or feeling might not make sense. {Hearticboy, Hearticenbie, Hearticgirl, Hearticnonbinary}

HEARTICBOY ♂ .... Masculine variation of Heartic.

HEARTICENBIE (Hearticnonbinary) .... Nonbinary variation of Heartic.

HEARTICGIRL ♀ .... Feminine variation of Heartic.

HEARTICNONBINARY (see Hearticenbie)

HELICGENDER .... Spiral-like.

HELIOGENDER .... Warm, burning.

HERMAIRIC .... A gender feeling all knowing, but still searching, growin, underlying tone of power and other worldly energy,

HERMITHYPIC .... Connected to video game Hermitcraft.

HIELBOY ♂ .... Masculine variation of Hielon.

HIELGIRL ♀ .... Feminine variation of Hielon.

HIELON .... Connected to ice, glaciers, or like ice, glaciers, might feel frozen in place for longer than usual and not returning to fluidity. {Hielboy, Hielgirl}

HIKARIFLUX .... A gender felt during peaceful or happier moments of heavy depression.

HIRCINIC .... Feeling human, non-human, other worldly energy.

HISTRIOGENDER .... Connected to one's Histrionic Personality Disorder, might change rapidly due to surroundings.

HOH-GENDER .... Connected to one's hearing loss, deafness.

HOLOGENDER .... Connected to being holographic.

HOTPINKGENDER .... Connected to color hot pink.

HEMIGENDER .... Half one gender, half another with one or both unidentifiable.

HETEROGENDER .... Connected to being heterosexual.

HIBERNALEMIAN .... Cozy, snowy.

HIPPIEGENDER .... Upbeat, passionate.

HOLIDELUSOGENDER .... Connected to delusions of being divine, holy, demonic, angelic, godly.

HOLLOWGENDER .... Connected to video game Hollow Knight, might be grimey, underground, infested, mystical aura.

HOLOGENDER .... Connected to holograms, or like a hologram.

HOMEYGENDER .... Comforting, warm.

HONEYCORIC .... Connected to honey.

HONEYGENDER .... Warm, protective, soft, innocent, finds comfort in others, like a blanket.

HOODIEGENDER .... Safe feeling, might be hiding something or feeling mysterious.

HORIZONGENDER .... Feeling distant, might be examined only with broad strokes and fuzzy detail.

HOROGENDER .... Changing over time with core feeling of gender remaining the same.

HORSECORIC .... Connected to horses.

HORSHUGENDER .... Feeling so extremely intense it begins to resemble its opposite binary gender.

HYCREATIA .... Wild, hyperactive, might be aggressive but not negatively.

HYDROGENDER .... Connected to water, or like water.

HYPERFIXGENDER (Passiogender) .... Might be connected to one's hyperfixations due to a mental disorder.

HYPERNURIX .... Connected to one's current hyperfixation due to a mental disorder.

HYPERSGENDER (Mealla) .... Connected one's hypersexuality.

HYSTERICAGENDER .... A gender when thought about makes one hysterical.

ICAEGENDER .... Animalistic, otherworldly, connected to psychic abilities.

ICEGENDER .... Cold, disconnected from emotions.

IDgender (Intellegender) .... Connected to one's intellectual disability.

IGNIAN .... Connected to campfires, roasting marshmallows, ghost stories.

IGNISGENDER .... Connected to fire, or has feelings of heat, brightness.

IGNOTUMFLUX (Ignotumfluid) .... Nonbinary, fluid, being inherently confusing due to one's depression or personality disorders.

IGNOTUMFLUID (see Ignotumflux)

IGNOTUMGENDER .... Nonbinary, being inherently confusing due to one's depression or personality disorders.

IJUSGENDER .... Connected to candles.

ILLUSOBOY ♂ .... Masculine variation of Illusogender.

ILLUSOGENDER .... Being a certain gender but feeling it is fake due to external influences. {Illusoboy, Illusogirl}

ILLUSOGIRL ♀ .... Feminine variation of Illusogender.

ILYAGENDER .... A gender feeling not male, female, neutral, Agender, nor any combination or derivation of them.

IMNIGENDER (see Anxiegender)

IMPERIGENDER .... Controllable, fluid.

IMPLAGENDER .... A gender one is never feeling satisfied with no matter how good the fit due to self-doubt which leads to compulsively searching for a better fit with any gender.

INBERGENDER .... Animalistic, otherworldly, connected to water.

INCERTAGENDER .... No true gender due to shaky sense of self from Borderline Personality Disorder.

INCOGNITASENSIUS .... A gender where one's true gender is unknown or non-existent but still identifying with a specific gender.

INDIGENDER .... Connected to being of Indigenous cultures and races.

INEFFABILLISIAN .... A gender unable to be explained other than it exists due to seemingly having no purpose.

INGENDER (Interagender, Intergenderless, Vacagender) .... Agender due to being intersex.

INKOPOD .... Connected to video game Splatoon.

INNOGENDER .... Not describable in words, unique to one's self but one knows and understands the gender clearly.

INSOMNIAGENDER .... Connected to one's insomnia.

INTAMINGENDER .... Connected to Liechtenstein based amusement ride manufacturer Intamin, might experience smooth yet fast highs, lows.

INTEGENDER (Amalgender, Mera; see Amalgagender)

INTELLEGENDER (see IDgender)

INTERAGENDER (Intergenderless, Vacagender; see Ingender)

INTER-ALIGNED .... Nonbinary, intersex.

INTERGENDER ⚥ .... Mixing male and female filling in space between genders.

INTERGENDERLESS (Interagender, Vacagender; see Ingender)

INTERNETEXPLORERGENDER .... Slow, clunky, has nostalgic feeling.

INTERNETGENDER .... Like primitive 1990's computer operating systems and internet websites.

INTERSEX .... Gender not identifying with one's medically assigned gender of male or female.

INVISIGENDER .... Being partially or fully invisible.

ISHIMONDIC .... Connected to Danganronpa novels.

ISOGENDER .... Intersex gender identifying with one's medically assigned gender chosen without input.

ITHYPHALLOI .... Assigned-female-at-birth who follows Greek god Dionysus.

JELLOGENDER .... Faint like it's covered with something preventing coming out into the open.

JELLYGENDER .... A gender rocking back and forth.

JELLYIC .... Connected to jelly beans.

JEWELGENDER .... Fluid, static, connected to gems not rocks.

JIGGLYGENDER .... Connected to character Jigglypuff of TV show Pokemon, might be mostly feminine, partly masculine, soothing, melodic.

JINGLEGENDER .... Connected to winter, or like winter.

JINNARUIAN ♂ .... Vaguely masculine, frosty, as thin as ice, hazy, might be connected to frost, snowy January mornings, winter, new beginnings.

JUGAGENDER .... Magical, mysterious.

JULIANIC .... Orderly, moments of chaos, other worldly energy.

JUPARETTIAN (Veusian) ♂♀ .... Fluid between Juparian and Lunettian.

JUPARIAN (Neptunian) ♂ .... Masculine variation of Mercurian.

JUXERA ♀ .... Similar to a girl but on a separate plane of living.

KAFEAN .... Connected to color brown, might be connected to soil, depth, ground, roots, trees.

KALICORIC .... Connected to Hindu goddess Kali.

KANDICORIC (Kandigender) .... Connected to Kandi bracelets and related items.

KANDIGENDER (see Kandicoric)

KANDIMANGA .... Bright, colorful.

KAWAIICORIC .... Connected to J-Pop and heavy metal Kawaiicore music and culture.

KHAOSGENDER .... Fast, connected to mayhem.

KIDCORIC .... Connected to bright colors, 90's culture, kid themes.

KIDDIECOASTERGENDER .... Like a kiddie rollercoaster with small highs, lows, doesn't go very fast.

KILRIAGENDER .... Like childhood memories.

KINGCORIC .... Connected to kings, might be masculine or feminine.

KINGENDER .... A gender defined only by one's kinship with a non-human species.

KINGGENDER ♂ .... Lofty, grandiose, might be majestic, bold, confident, imposing, commanding.

KITCORIC .... Connected to neon colors, rainbows, accessories.

KITTENGENDER (Kittycoric, Kittygender, Nyagender; see Catgender)

KITTYBOYGENDER .... A gender for one who is human and cat due to autism.

KITTYCORIC (Kittengender, Kittygender, Nyagender; see Catgender)

KITTYGENDER (Kittycoric, Kittengender, Nyagender; see Catgender)

KNIGHTCORIC .... Connected to knights.

KORAALAIC .... Connected to colors orange, coral, yellow, gold, might be connected to coral reefs, oceans.

KUIPERIAN .... Fluid between soft celestial energies.

KUNIGENDER .... A gender obstructed due to trauma, might change based on the situation.

KYNARIC .... Connected to air, other worldly energy.

KYNIGENDER (see Genderinimicus)

LACHRYMOSIAN .... Connected to coldness, quietness, night.

LAETUSGENDER .... Dark, eurphoric.

LAMINGENDER (Stratogender) .... A gender with multiple layered genders.

LANTERNAER (Leukogender) .... Brightly shining.

LAPIDEGENDER .... Connected to rocks, gems.

LARUAGENDER .... Animalistic, otherworldly, connected to ghosts.

LAUNDRIAROMATIC .... Like smells of clean laundry.

LAYTONGENDER .... Connected to video game Professor Layton, might be connected to adventure, puzzles, archaology.

LAZULIGENDER .... A gender that changed to heal from trauma, might be repressed trauma.

LEGOGENDER .... Feeling built from another gender.

LENSGENDER .... A confusing gender only understood by those observing and not by one's self.

LESBIANGENDER ♀ .... When being a woman attracted to women is so intrinsically connected to one's gender the two can't be separated.

LEUKOGENDER (see Lanternaer)

LIBIDOGENDER .... Connected to one's libido, sex drive.

LIBRAFEMININE ♀ .... Feminine variation of Libragender.

LIBRAGENDER .... Being Agender but with strong connection to another gender with Agender more prominent. {Librafeminine, Libramasculine}

LIBRAMASCULINE ♂ .... Masculine variation of Libragender.

LICORIYIC .... Connected to licorice.

LIGHTCORIC (Lightgender) .... Connected to light, might be like light, might contain all colors simultaneously.

LIGHTGENDER (see Lightcoric)

LIGNESOLUM .... Connected to robotics, technology, nostalgia, color gray.

LIGNUMGENDER .... Fluid, connected to wood, lumber, trees.

LILAGENDER .... Connected to color lilac.

LINGUISTINGENDER .... Connected to language, linguistics, might be connected to literature and writing.

LIPSIGENDER .... A gender triggering depression when thought about.

LITHIGENDER .... Static gender feeling more intense during manic episodes, less intense during depressive episodes due to bipolar disorder.

LITTLEFLUID (see Ageregender)

LIZARDGENDER .... Connected to lizards, might be connected to Doors singer Jim Morrison nicknamed the Lizard King.

LOCATIAGENDER .... Connected to general non-specific locations.

LOCHBOY ♂ .... Masculine variation of Lochen.

LOCHEN .... Fluid, Multi-Gender, connected to lakes, like a lake. {Lochboy, Lochenby, Lochgirl}

LOCHENBY .... Nonbinary variation of Lochen.

LOCHGIRL ♀ .... Feminine variation of Lochen.

LOCOBOY ♂ .... Masculine variation of Locogender.

LOCOGENDER .... Connected to general specific locations, might be like specific locations. {Locoboy, Locogirl, Locononbinary}

LOCOGIRL ♀ .... Feminine variation of Locogender.

LOCONONBINARY .... Nonbinary variation of Locogender.

LOCUN .... Connected to starry skies, childhood, dreams.

LOLIGENDER ♀ .... Girl-like, child-like.

LOLITAGENDER ♀ .... Connected to Lolita fashion that mixes cuteness with Victorian clothing.

LORAGENDER (Ballorgender; see Balloragender)

LOVECORIC .... Connected to love.

LUCKYGENDER .... Lucky feeling.

LUDOGENDER .... A gender mirroring other people by trying on their genders.

LUDOSBOY♂ .... Masculine variation of Ludosgender.

LUDOSGENDER .... Connected to playing cards, dice, gambling equipment. {Ludosboy, Ludosenby, Ludosgirl}

LUDOSENBY .... Nonbinary variation of Ludosgender.

LUDOSGIRL♀ .... Feminine variation of Ludosgender.

LUDUGENDER .... Distant, separate, difficult to find, like a video game.

LUMENIAN .... With a glowing feeling.

LUMEVIR ♂ .... When lacking gender distinction is central to one's identity.

LUMINOGENDER .... Like a ray of light shining through a window.

LUMNIC (see Hallowgender)

LUNARIAGENDER .... Connected to 2020 movie Over The Moon.

LUNETTIAN ♀ .... Feminine variation of Mercurian.

LURIDGENDER .... Connected to pastel colors, dark emotions.

LUXAER .... Light, misty.

LUXIAN .... Happy, connected to rainbows, sunshine.

MAGICORIC .... Connected to magic, illusions.

MACHINEGENDER (Mechangender, Mechanigender, Mechgender) .... Like a robot, android, AI, man-made sentient mechanical being, might be due to mental disorder, might feel stronger connection to robots, disconnected from humans. {Mechanboy, Mechangirl}

MAGICAGENDER .... Connected to Japanese Anime series Puella Magi Madoka Magica, might be deceptively sweet and innocent at first glance.

MAGIGENDER .... Mostly one gender with rest is something else. {Magiboy, Magigendernonbinary, Magigirl, Magigenderfaun, Magiguy, Magiman, Maginonbinary}

MAGIBOY (Magiguy, Magiman) ♂ .... Masculine variation of Magigender.

MAGIGENDERFAUN (Magigirl) ♀ .... Feminine variation of Magigender.

MAGIGENDERNONBINARY (Maginonbinary) .... Nonbinary variation of Magigender.

MAGIGIRL (see Magigenderfaun) ♀

MAGIGUY (Magiman; see Magiboy) ♂

MAGIMAN (Magiguy; see Magiboy) ♂

MAGINONBINARY (see Magigendernonbinary)

MAGNETGENDER (Dustbunnygender, see Cumulogender)

MAGNIFEIC .... Large, powerful.

MAGSOLUM .... Connected to time, literature, the sun, color magenta.

MAIUIAN .... Toasty, calming, connected to flowers, summer rain, meadows, wind.

MALACATHIC .... A gender feeling stronger when rejected by others, other worldy energy.

MALAGENDER .... Connected to one's maladaptive daydreaming.

MALE .... Social construct related to masculinity

MALE-TO-FEMALE (MTF) ♂♀ .... Assigned male at birth but now female.

MALINEGENDER (see Bi-vir)

MANERIUMUS .... Rickety, old, yet comforting.

MANUGENDER ♂ .... Nonbinary with some elements of masculinity.

MARAIC .... Loving, compassionate, other worldly energy.

MAREIC .... Connected to character Nightmare Fredbear of video game Five Nights At Freddy's, might be haunting, nightmare-like, devouring, cruel, dangerous, mechanical.

MARIOGENDER .... Connected to characters from Nintendo video games.

MARONIC .... Connected to passion, affection, attention, candy, color maroon.

MARSEAN ♂ .... Juparian, Mercurian, Plutoian.

MARSIAFLUID .... Fluid between coric genders.

MARZUIAN .... Like spring, flowerly, lightly frosted, thin, calming.

MASCAGENUS CHRISTIAN ♂ .... Christian, nonbinary, connected to masculinity.

MASCFLUID ♂ .... Fluid gender restricted to masculine genders.

MASCFLUIDFLUX ♂ .... Masculine variation of Fluidflux.

MASCGENDER ♂ .... Nonbinary but masculine in nature.

MASC-TENEBRAIC ♂ .... Masculine variation of Tenebraic.

MASOGENDER .... Connected to non-sexual pain and humiliation towards one's self.

MATHGENDER .... Connected to math, numbers.

MAUVAISOLUM .... Connected to flowers, poison, growth, trickery, color magenta.

MAVERIVIR .... Part male, part maverique.

MCSQUIDGENDER .... Connected to squids, ocean from video game Minecraft.

MEADOWCORIC .... Connected to meadows.

MEALLA (see Hypersgender)

MECHANBOY ♂ .... Masculine variation of Machinegender.

MECHANENBY .... Nonbinary variation of Machinegender.

MECHANGENDER (Mechanigender, Mechgender; see Machinegender)

MECHANGIRL ♀ .... Feminine variation of Machinegender.

MECHANIGENDER (Mechangender, Mechgender; see Machinegender)

MECHGENDER (Mechangender, Mechanigender; see Machinegender)

MEDCORIC .... Connected to medicine, doctors.

MEDIANFLUID .... Every part of one's personality is different genders.

MENHERAIC (Neurogender) .... Connected to one's mental disorders, might be connected to the mind in general.

MEPHIC .... A gender filling one with anxiety about not knowing it, has underlying feelings of power, other worldly energy.

MEOWGENDER .... Connected to older cats.

MEOWTIANGENDER (Nyaliengender) .... Catgender, Aliengender.

MERA (Amalgender, Integender; see Amalgagender)

MERCURIAN ♂♀ .... Nonbinary, connected to a void with changing intensities of soft celestial energy either feminine or non-hyper masculine. {Juparian, Lunettian, Neptunian}

MERIDIC .... Connected to Earth energy.

MERJUPARIAN (see Erisian) ♂

MERMAIDCORIC .... Connected to mermaids, mermen, merfolk.

MERUONIC .... Evil, destructive to other genders, other worldy power.

METALCORIC (Metallarian) .... Connected to metals.

METALLARIAN (see Metalcoric)

METALLIGENDER .... Connected to precious metals.

METAPHURIAC .... When one's gender identity and gender metaphor are identical.

MEWGENDER .... Connected to kittens.

MEWIC .... Connected to character Mew of TV show Pokemon.

MEXGENDER .... Animalistic, otherworldly, connected to bugs.

MIDBINARY (see Exobinary)

MICROSOFTEDGEGENDER .... A gender feeling in the way.

MINECRAFTGENDER .... Conntected to video game Minecraft.

MINEGENDER .... Connected to mining aspect of video game Minecraft, might search for things, use them, move on.

MINEHYPIC .... Connected to video game Minecraft.

MIRRORGENDER .... Changing to blend with people around one.

MISTIGENDER .... Like fog.

MOLLIGENDER .... Soft, subtle, subdued.

MOLLIVGENDER .... Having more than one gender but being unmotivated to discover each of them, or knowing more than one gender exists makes one question one's self and stick with labels that work versus better suited ones.

MOLTIC .... Connected to character Molten Freddy of video game Five Nights At Freddy's, might be broken down, hysterical, small, dangerous, mechanical.

MOMCORIC .... Connected to mothers, mothering.

MONSGENDER .... Animalistic, otherworldly, connected to rocks.

MONSTERBOY ♂ .... Masculine variation of Monstergender.

MONSTERGENDER .... Having a weak sense or no sense of gender with feelings of inhumanity replacing the missing sense of gender. {Monsterboy, Monstergirl}

MONSTERGIRL ♀ .... Feminine variation of Monstergender.

MONSTROGENDERVOID .... Essentially no gender with what little gender exists feeling inhuman, monstrous.

MOONCORIC .... Connected to the moon, might be connected to moons in general.

MORBALIC .... Feeling trapped on a separate plane of living, other worldly energy.

MOSSCORIC .... Connected to moss, other fungi.

MOUNTAINCORIC .... Connected to mountains.

MOUSEGENDER .... Small, soft, hiding, sneaking around, might be connected to mice.

MTF (see Male-To-Female) ♂♀

MULTIFENEF .... Multiple Five Nights At Freddy's video game based genders simultaneously or separate.

MULTI-GENDER (Omnigender, Polygender) .... Multiple genders simultaneously or separately.

MULTIOCULAEC .... Connected to having multiple eyes, or wanting multiple eyes.

MUSICCORIC (see Cadensgender)

MUSICGENDER (see Audiogender)

MULTAGENUS .... Christian, Multi-Gender.

MYTHOGENDER .... Connected to mythology.

NAMEGENDER (Egogender; see Charagender)

NAMERIC .... tries to be repulsive, other worldly energy.

NANOBOY ♂ .... Masculine variation of Nanogender.

NANOGENDER (Subgender) .... Very small part one gender, mostly something else {Nanoboy, Nanogirl, Subboy, Subgirl}

NANOGIRL ♀ .... Feminine variation of Nanogender.

NARGENDER .... Connected to fire, heat, excitement, determination, high energy, might become frightening with angered.

NARKISSENBY (Narkissinb) .... Nonbinary variation of Narkissigender.

NARKISSIBOI (Narkissiboy) ♂ .... Masculine variation of Narkissigender.

NARKISSIBOY (see Narkissiboi) ♂

NARKISSIGENDER .... Egotistical, arrogant, needing praise, lofty. {Narkissenby, Narkissiboi, Narkissiboy, Narkissigirl, Narkissinb, Narkissixirl}

NARKISSIGIRL (Narkissixirl) ♀ .... Feminine variation of Narkissigender.

NARKISSINB (see Narkissenby)

NARKISSIXIRL (see Narkissigirl) ♀

NATIOGENDER (Nial) ....Connected to one's nation, might be connected to one's state, might be connected to one's ethnic group.

NATURECORIC (Naturengender, see Biogender)

NATURENGENDER (Naturecoric; see Biogender)

NAUFRAGIUMGENDER .... An abandoned gender, like a shipwreck vanishing and then being rediscovered later.

NAVICORIC .... Connected to novel House Of Leaves.

NEBBIABOY ♂ .... Masculine variation of Foggender.

NEBBIAGENDER (Genderfog, Gendervague; see Foggender)

NEBBIAGIRL ♀ .... Feminine variation of Foggender.

NEBGENDER (Vaguegender) .... A gender where one is unable to pinpoint the exact gender or understand it due to mental disorder. {Vagueboy, Vaguegirl}

NECROGENDER .... A non dead or nonexistent gender.

NEGAGENDER .... Connected to negative symptoms of one's schizophrenia.

NEKEIVAH ♀ .... Jewish, assigned female at birth, Cisgender.

NEONCORIC (Neonic) .... Connected to neon, neon lights.

NEONGENDER .... Colorful where one's gender or parts of it shine brightly and distract one's self.

NEOION .... Connected to bright neon colors of the 1980's, might be connected to the finsexual flag colors.

NEONIC (see Neoncoric)

NEPTUNIAN (see Juparian) ♂

NEPTUNUN .... Like oceans or seas.

NETBOY ♂ .... Masculine variation of Netgender.

NETGENDER (Netqueer) .... A gender expressed more frequently online than face-to-face. {Netboy, Netgirl, Netnonbinary, Netqueer}

NETGIRL ♀ .... Feminine variation of Netgender.

NETNONBINARY .... Nonbinary variation of Netgender.

NETQUEER (see Netgender)

NETSCAPEGENDER .... Incredibly old, created in a strange way.

NETTAIAN .... Tropical, loving, connected to summer, warm weather, oceans, coconuts, beaches, seashells, mixing all tropical feeling genders.

NEUROGENDER (see Menheraic)

NEUTRAGENUS CHRISTIAN .... Christian, nonbinary, neutral, might be androgynous.

NEUT-TENEBRAIC .... Neutral variation of Tenebraic.

NEUTROIS .... Having a neutral gender, or having a lack of gender which leads to feeling neutral or Agender.

NEUTROIX .... Neutrois due to being Intersex.

NEUTROVIR ♂ .... Part male, part Neutrois.

NIAL (see Natiogender)

NIDOGENDER .... Fragrant, full of richness.

NIGHTMACORIC .... Connected to nightmares, bad dreams.

NIGHTMIC .... Connected to character Nightmare Freddy of video game Five Nights At Freddy's, might haunting, nightmarelike, cruel, dangerous, mechanical.

NISGENDER .... Animalistic, otherworldly, connected to fire.

NISSENE .... Soft, comforting, connected to pixies, gold dust, sleep, magic.

NITORICINE .... Fluffy, soft, kindhearted.

NIVEUSBAONIC .... Fluid, connected to snowmen, dead trees, snow, ice, rebirth, bleakness, coldness, warm homes, fireplaces.

NOCTFLUID .... Fluid between night related genders.

NOCTURNIC .... Dark, underlying feeling of power, other worldly energy.

NOIRGENDER (Gothgender; see Gothcoric)

NOKORIBIC (see Favillaric)

NONBINARY (Enbie, Gender Nonconforming, Genderqueer, Gender Variant, Third Gender, X-Gender; see Cogender)

NON-GENDERED (Genderfree, Genderless; see Agender)

NOSTALGIACORIC .... Connected to nostalgia.

NOUNGENDER .... A gender best described by a noun.

NOVIGENDER .... A gender indescribable using existing language due to its complex and unique nature.

NOWOMAGENDER .... Being all possible genders except female.

NOXGENDER .... Animalistic, otherworldly, connected to darkness.

NOXIAN .... Connected to darkness, might be connected to night.

NOXIGENDER ♂♀ .... Mostly male, partially nonbinary with some female.

NOXNIDORIAN .... Connected to night, smells of the night.

NUAGESOLUM .... Soft, connected to neutrality, fog, stars, the sun, color purple.

NUBESVAGUM .... Very vague due to external force, like weather on cloudy days.

NUITSOLUM .... Dark, connected to power, space, moons, empty voids, color purple.

NUJIANA .... Gentle, calming, colorful, loving, fluid, connected to rainbows, summer, rain, bright colors.

NULL GENDER .... Without a masculine or feminine gender, might not be neutral.

NUTRIENCEGENDER (Foodgender, Gastrongender; see Foodcoric)

NUVEMBRIAN .... Fading out, small, changes rapidly, connected to autumn, cold weather, snow.

NYALIENGENDER (see Meowtiangender)

NYAGENDER (Kittengender, Kittycoric, Kittygender; see Catgender)

NYCTOGENDER .... Being pure darkness.

OBJECTUMGENDER .... Connected to one's special objects being autistic.

OBLIFEMININE ♀ .... Feminine variation of Obligender.

OBLIGENDER .... Connected to one's assigned gender at birth. {Oblifeminine, Oblimasculine}

OBLIMASCULINE ♂ .... Masculine variation of Olbigender.

OBLIVIGENDER .... A gender when one doesn't understand what gender is or what it means to be any gender.

OCDBOY ♂ .... Masculine variation of OCDgender.

OCDGENDER .... Connected to one's OCD.

OCDGIRL ♀ .... Feminine variation of OCDgender.

OCDNONBINARY .... Nonbinary variation of OCDgender.

OCUGENDER .... A gender only present when looked for.

OFFBINARY (Exterbinary; see Abinary)

OFFGENDER (Quasixenogender) .... Having an off feeling, might be like an alien imitating human gender.

OGLIGENDER .... Two to five genders.

OMNICORIC .... Connected to the omnisexual flag colors.

OMNIGENDER (Polygender; see Multi-Gender)

ONCAGENDER .... Connection to jaguars.

ONEIROGENDER .... Being Agender but with recurring fantasies and daydreams of being a certain gender without gender dysphoria or desire to actually be that gender.

OPALIC .... Connected to opals, might have a smooth exterior, be fragile.

OPERAGENDER .... Connected to Opera music and culture, might feel unused but works well.

OPPOGENDER .... Two or more contradictory genders simultaneously or separately.

OPSCUGENDER .... Dark, murky, hard to see and describe.

OPTIGENDER .... Connected to eyes, vision problems, perfect vision.

ORANGEGENDER .... Connected to color orange.

ORBGENDER .... Round, without edges.

ORIENTATIONGENDER .... A gender so intrinsically connected to one's sexual orientation the two can't be separated.

OSSEUSNE .... Connected to skeletons or bones, Halloween, spirits, might be bare or barely there.

OSTOSGENDER .... Soothing, feeling distant, like childhood memories remembered clearly and calmly.

OTHERGENDER .... A gender other than male or female.

OURANIAN .... Plutoian, Mercurian.

PALUN .... Like a swamp or marsh.

PANCORIC .... Connected to the pansexual flag colors, or identifying as all Coric genders.

PANFLUX .... Being all genders, but might change to gender feeling more right.

PANGENDER .... Having every gender in one's own culture simultaneously or separately.

PANICGENDER .... Fluid, changing due to one's panic attacks.

PANTECHNICUM (Gendertech, Techcoric, Technogender; see Cybergender)

PAPERGENDER .... Thin, fragile, like a blank piece of paper.

PARADELUSOGENDER .... Connected to one's paranoid delusions.

PARADNURIX .... Connected to one's paranoia due to ADHD.

PARADOXGENDER .... Being all genders at different times with no overlap.

PARAMEBOY ♂ .... Masculine variation of Paramegender.

PARAMEGENDER .... Connected to events in one's dreams, being someone in your dreams, might be like seeing the world from the dreams. {Parameboy, Paramegirl, Paramenonbinary}

PARAMEGIRL ♀ .... Feminine variation of Paramegender.

PARAMENONBINARY .... Nonbinary variation of Paramegender.

PAROREXGENDER .... Connected to one's Parorexia, Hyperorexia.

PAROUGENDER (see Fabricgender)

PARTYGENDER .... Connected to parties.

PASOFTGENDER .... Soft, playful, connected to pastels, hearts, might be androgynous.

PASSIMLIX .... Chaotic, bouncy, euphoric feelings, hard to pin down.

PASSIOGENDER (see Hyperfixgender)

PASTELBLUEGENDER .... Connected to color pastel blue.

PASTELCORIC .... Connected to Pastel-core music and culture.

PASTELGENDER .... Connected to pastel colors.

PASTELGREENGENDER .... Connected to color pastel green.

PASTELGOTHCORIC .... Connected to pastel goth scene.

PASTELYELLOWGENDER .... Connected to color pastel yellow.

PASTGENDER .... A gender feeling like it reincarnated, has past lives maybe identifiable.

PASUGOSGENDER .... Being pastel and goth, but not pastel goth.

PATIGENDER .... A gender one doesn't like but identify with it anyways as a placeholder for one's true gender.

PEACHGENDER .... Little fuzzy, soft, easy to hurt, like eating peaches.

PEGASUS (Earth Pony, Unicorn; see Ponygender)

PENDO-AGENDER (Pendogender, Xumgender) .... A gender one is never feeling satisfied with no matter how good the fit due to self-doubt which leads to compulsively searching for a better fit with no gender. {Pendojuxera}

PENDOGENDER (Xumgender; see Pendo-Agender)

PENDOJUXERA ♀ .... Feminine variation of Pendo-Agender.

PEOPLEGENDER .... Connected to a certain person, or type of person.

PEPPERMINTYIC .... Connected to peppermint.

PERIGENDER .... A gender identifying with gender but not as a gender.

PERIDGENDER .... Like the gem peridot, might be connected to healing powers, curing depression, color green.

PERIWINKLEYN .... Connected to color periwinkle.

PERIWINKLIAN .... Beautiful, calm gender, connected to color periwinkle, might be connected to ice, water, serenity.

PEROGENDER .... A gender wanting to be a certain gender but not being that gender.

PERYIC .... Disorderly despite efforts to organize, other worldy energy.

PEWT .... Nonbinary gender with androgynous presentation.

PHANPHENDER .... Connected to character Phanpy of TV show Pokemon.

PHANTIC .... Connected to character Phantom Freddy of video game Five Nights At Freddy's, might be burnt, ghost-like, hallucinative, dangerous, mechanical.

PIANOGENDER .... Connected to pianos.

PICHUGENDER .... Connected to characte Pichu of TV show Pokemon, might be small, feeling fuzzy with electrical charge.

PIGGENDER .... Connected to pigs, might be like a pig.

PIKAGENDER .... Connected to character Pikachu of TV show Pokemon, might feel fuzzy with electrical charge.

PINKCORE (Pinkgender; see Genderpink)

PINKGENDER (Pinkcore; see Genderpink)

PIRATECORIC .... Connected to pirates.

PISCIBOY ♂ .... Masculine variation of Piscin.

PISCIENBY .... Nonbinary variation of Piscin.

PISCIGIRL ♀ .... Feminine variation of Piscin.

PISCIN .... Connected to swimming pools, or like swimming pools, might not be connected to swimming. {Pisciboy, Piscienby, Piscigirl}

PIXELBOY ♂ .... Masculine variation of Pixelgender.

PIXELGENDER .... Identifying minimally as one gender, plus another. {Pixelboy, Pixelgirl, Pixelnonbinary}

PIXELGIRL ♀ .... Feminine variation of Pixelgender.

PIXELNONBINARY .... Nonbinary variation of Pixelgender.

PLANTCORE (Plantcoric) .... Connected to plants.

PLANTCORIC (see Plantcore)

PLUITOMVILIC .... Connected to autumn rain, cities in the rain, laziness, melancholy.

PLURISGENUS .... A gender complicated and connected to being Trans.

PLUSHYIC .... Connected to stuffed plush toys.

PLUTOIAN .... Connected to a void but lacking some celestial energy.

PLUVBOY ♂ .... Masculine variation of Pluvian.

PLUVGIRL ♀ .... Feminine variation of Pluvian.

PLUVIAN .... Fluid like rain or another form of precipitation, might be connected to rain. {Pluvboy, Pluvgirl}

POKEGENDER (Pokeic, Pokemongender) .... Connected to TV show Pokemon.

POKEIC (Pokemongender; see Pokegender)

POKEMONGENDER (Pokeic; see Pokegender)

POLARBEARGENDER .... Connected to polar bears.

POLYCORIC .... Connected to the polysexual flag colors.

POLYGENDER (Omnigender; see Multi-Gender)

POMOGENDER (see Genderweird)

PONYGENDER (Earth Pony, Pegasus, Unicorn) .... Connected to ponies.

PORTAEGENDER .... Composed of various parts of many sizes.

POSIGENDER .... Connected to positive symptoms of one's schizophrenia.

POSTBOY ♂ .... Masculine variation of Postgender.

POSTGENDER .... A gender moving away from identifying as a specific gender. {Postboy, Postgirl}

POSTGIRL ♀ .... Feminine variation of Postgender.

PREBOY ♂ .... Masculine variation of Pregender.

PREGENDER .... A gender moving to identify as a specific gender. {Preboy, Preboy}

PREGIRL ♀ .... Feminine variation of Pregender.

PRESENTGENDER .... Revealing itself as a surprise.

PRESQUEGENDER ♂♀ .... Neutral, connected to femininity and masculinity.

PREZBOY ♂ .... Masculine variation of Prezgender.

PREZGIRL ♀ .... Feminine variation of Prezgender.

PRINCECORIC (Princegender) ♂ .... Masculine variation of Princengender.

PRINCEGENDER (see Princecoric) ♂

PRINCENGENDER (Pringender) ♂♀ .... Soft, prim, ethereal gender, majestic, imposing, grandiose, might be connected to princes, princesses. {Princecoric, Princesscoric, Princessgender, Princegender}

PRINCESSCORIC (Princessgender) ♀ .... Feminine variation of Princengender.

PRINCESSGENDER (see Princesscoric) ♀

PRINGENDER (see Princengender) ♂♀

PRISMGENDER .... Fluid, connected to one's hyperfixations due to ADHD, might be impulsively and spontaneously changing with an inability to settle with one gender for long periods of time.

PRISMAGENDER .... Best described with all colors of a rainbow.

PRIVUMGENDER .... Connected to one's Antisocial Personality Disorder.

PRONGENDER .... Dependent on one's preferred pronouns.

PROXVIR ♂ .... Similar to a boy but on a separate plane of living.

PSYCHOGENDER .... A gender only understood in context of one's psychotic disorder, might be inconsistent, hard to understand, might feel disconnected from reality.

PSYCHOREXGENDER .... Connected to one's schizophrenia, psychosexual development.

PUFFGENDER .... Connected to pufferfish or similar fish.

PUNQUE .... Connected to Punk music and culture.

PUPCATGENDER .... Connected to dogs, cats.

PUPPETIC .... Connected to puppets, marionettes.

PUPPYCORIC (see Dogcoric)

PURGENDER (Purplegender) .... Connected to color purple.

PURITYGENDER .... Pure, untainted, connected to roses.

PURPLEGENDER (see Purgender)

PURPUSOLUM .... Connected to nonconformity, fashion, royalty, color purple.

PURRGENDER .... Small, nimble, restless, tired, like a cat.

PUTEARIN (Putenain) .... Connected to pillows, good night's rest, dark rooms, the moon, stars, might be hollow, cool.

PUTENAIN (see Putearin)

PUZZLEGENDER .... Pieced together, might be missing pieces.

PUZZLEIC .... Connected to puzzles of any sort.

PYREXGENDER .... Connected to one's raised body temperature, fever.

QIRL ♀ .... Nonbinary, people of color

QUADGENDER .... Four distinct genders simultaneously or separately.

QUASIXENIC (Xenogender; see Aliagender)

QUASIXENOGENDER (see Offgender)

QUEENCORIC .... Connected to queens, might be masculine or feminine.

QUEENGENDER ♀ .... Lofty, grandiose, might be bold, majestic, imposing, commanding, confident.

QUEERCORIC .... Connected to Queercore punk music and culture.

QUOIBINARY .... A gender where the concept of gender binary is confusing, inaccessible or inapplicable to one's self.

QUOIGENDER .... Feeling gender identity or existing gender terms don't apply or are nonsensical to one's self, or having a complicated relationship with gender. {Quoivir}

QUOIVIR ♂ .... Masculine variation of Quoigender.

QUPHA ♀ .... Being a woman but not girl, might not be feminine in any traditional way, might be loud, large, but still soft, warm.

RADIOGENDER .... Connected to radios, radio broadcasts.

RAETBOY ♂ .... Masculine variation of Raetgender.

RAETGENDER .... Connected to rats. {Raetboy, Raetgirl}

RAETGIRL ♀ .... Feminine variation of Raetgender.

RAIGENDER .... Connected to character Raichu of TV show Pokemon, might feel fuzzy with electrical charge.

RAINBOWCORIC (Rainbowgender) .... Fluid, connected to rainbows, rainbow themed things.

RAINBOWGENDER (see Rainbowcoric)

RAINCORIC .... Connected to rain.

RAPCORIC .... Connected to Rap music and culture.

RAUMATAGENDER .... A gender feeling non-existent due to trama, might be fluid.

RAVECORIC (Ravercoric) .... Connected to Rave music and culture.

RAVERCORIC (see rRvecoric)

RAYOCIAN .... Fast paced, connected to summer, like air after a storm.

RAZORGENDER .... Sharp, swiftly moving.

REBIS .... A gender transcending idea of gender as binary.

REBRUSOLUM .... Connected to fire, the sun, summer, color red.

REDCORIC (Redgender) .... Connected to color red.

REDGENDER (see redcoric)

REGISGENDER .... Lofty, grandiose, nonbinary, might be bold, majestic, imposing, commanding, confident.

REGREGENDER .... Hard to identify due to age regression.

REGRESSGENDER .... A gender only present during age regression.

RELATIONGENDER (Relatishigender, Relatishipgender) .... Connected to certain feelings of attraction towards someone.

RELATISHIGENDER (Relatishipgender; see Relationgender)

RELATISHIPGENDER (Relatishigender; see Relatoingender)

RELIGIGENDER .... Connected to religion, might not be religious.

RENCGENDER .... A gender confusing and infuriating leading to impulsively collecting labels looking for a good fit due to Borderline Personality Disorder.

RENGENDER .... Connected to character Ren Amamiya/Joker of video game Persona 5, might be a leader, mischievous, caring, admirable, brave.

REOSOLUM .... Connected to demons, scales, moons, dragons, color black.

REPPERIOGENDER .... In the spotlight, or might act like a spotlight.

REPRIGENDER .... Connected to one's repression of themselves or pretending to be someone else due to past trauma.

RERUMBOY ♂ .... Masculine variation of Rerumgender.

RERUMGENDER .... A gender easier expressed over the internet than face-to-face. {Rerumboy, Rerumgirl, Rerumnonbinary}

RERUMGIRL ♀ .... Feminine variation of Rerumgender

RERUMNONBINARY .... Nonbinary variation of Rerumgender.

RETOURNERSOLUM .... Connected to power, farming, fashion, colors green, magenta.

RETROANE .... Busy, flamboyant, noisy, bright, like a mall in the 1980's, might be eventually found useless and abandoned.

REVERENTIAGENUS CHRISTIANS .... Christian, nonbinary, connected to femininity, masculinity, neutrality, might be androgynous.

RHODONITIAN ♀ .... Feminine gender but more neutral.

RION .... Multi-Gender like a river, might be connected to rivers.

RIXAGENDER .... Animalistic, otherworldly, connected to fighting.

ROBOTGENDER .... Feeling human in a very basic way, more robotic, might be due to mental disorder.

ROCKCORIC .... Connected to rocks not gems.

ROCKIC (Staric) .... Connected to character Rockstar Freddy of video game Five Nights At Freddy's, might be fresh, rebranded, musical, center of attention, with mailicious intent, greedy, dangerous, mechanical.

ROGOGENDER .... Animalistic, otherworldly, connected to glitches.

ROMANCECORIC .... Connected to romance.

ROSEASOLUM .... Connected to love, doves, stars, color pink.

ROSECORIC .... Connected to roses.

ROSGENDER .... Like morning dew in the air in the outdoors.

ROSSUINE .... Connected to blood, death, heat, passion, color red.

ROX (Roxgender) .... A gender fluid based on one's happiness.

ROXGENDER (see Rox)

RPGcoric .... Connected to role playing games.

RUBYGENDER ♂ .... Fluid, connected to rubies.

RUSTICORUMIAN .... Heavily rustic, cozy, connected to autumn, or like windy autumn days with leaves blowing on country lanes, might vanish after a few days.

RUSTICUSGENDER .... Composed of few large parts, independent.

RUUSUOAN .... Connected to colors rose, pink, magenta, might be connected to sunsets, sunrises, jewels, love, music, beauty.

SADCORIC .... Connected to sadness, depression.

SAFARIGENDER .... A gender hard to use.

SALMACIAN (Bigential; see Aphrodisian) ♂♀

SANGUISFLUID .... Fluid, thick, moving slowly, might cover other genders like blood.

SANTOIK .... Connected to being a ghost via slow, deathly, having feelings of floating.

SAPPHICGENDER ♀ .... Female gender with an attraction towards females where the gender and sexual orientation are completely intertwined.

SAPPHIREGENDER ♀ .... Connected to sapphires.

SAPPHOGENDER ♀ .... A gender only experiencing femininity through one's attraction to woman or female oriented genders.

SARIS ♂♀ .... Jewish, assigned male at birth, Trans.

SATURNIAN ♂♀ .... Nonbinary, fluctuating soft celestial masculine and feminine energy.

SAUDADEIC .... Distant gender one feels nostalgic and melancholic towards.

SAVMYSTERIUS ♂ .... Fluid, feeling shrouded in fog, hard to define, might be connected to crystals, forests, stars, death, old gods, demons, angels, fae.

SCANSIOGENDER .... A gender always rising.

SCATTERGENDER .... Feeling scattered.

SCHIZIC (Skhizeingender) .... Connected to one's schizophrenia, hard to understand.

SCHOOLCORIC (see Educoric)

SCIGENDER .... Connected to science.

SCORPIFLUID .... Fluid between two or more unknown genders.

SCORPIGENDER .... Mysterious, very difficult to understand as many labels vaguely fit but none fully describe it.

SEACORIC .... Connected to the sea.

SEAFOAMINA .... Vague, like it was lost like a shipwreck.

SEAGENDER .... Connected to seas, marine life.

SEPULTUSGENDER .... Deep, buried, cool.

SERONGENDER .... Like a very squishy ball.

SEXYGENDER .... Incredibly sexy.

SEZIONEGENDER .... Heavily divided or sectioned into pieces but making a whole.

SHADIC .... Connected to Slim Shady the character created by rapper Eminem with strong intrusive thoughts of violent or sexual nature.

SHADOWGENDER .... A gender separated from one's self.

SHELLFEMININE ♂♀ .... Masculine shell and a feminine core.

SHELLMASCULINE ♂♀ .... Feminine shell and a masculine core.

SHEOGORIC .... Wild, unpredictable, underlying feeling of power, other worldly energy.

SIDERODROMOGENDER .... Connected to trains.

SIMGENDER .... Connected to Sim games.

SIMUGENDER .... Like living in a simulation of the world.

SISLOGENDER (SLgender) .... Connected to video game Five Nights At Freddy's: Sister Location, might only be felt when playing game, might feel trapped in an unsatisfying body, stressed, being watched.

SITTEMBRIAN .... Slow, calming, connected to autumn, falling leaves, mountains, cool weather.

SKHIZEINGENDER (see Schizic)

SLgender (see Sislogender)

SMEAGENDER .... Connected to character Smeagol/Gollum from The Lord Of The Rings novels, might not feel quite human, small, animalistic, controlling, dark, weak, old.

SLIMIC .... Connected to Slim Shady the character created by rapper Eminem.

SMOOTHPEANUTBUTTERIC .... Connected to smooth peanut butter.

SHADEND .... Being a shadow, or in a shadow or darkness.

SHAMPOOIUM .... Sudsy like shampoo, making other genders feel clean.

SHIPWRECKIAN .... Connected to shipwrecks, deep sea, warm ocean water, color blue.

SILKGENDER .... Only felt in presence of silk.

SILLYGENDER .... Connected to clowns, kids, trauma.

SINEGENUS .... Christian, no gender.

SISSY ♂ .... <u>Assigned</u> male at birth but presenting feminine, or identifying female, or androgynous nonbinary.

SKULLCORIC .... Connected to skulls, might be connected to Halloween, might be connected to medicine.

SKYGENDER .... Connected to video game Sky: Children of the Light.

SLEEPYCORIC (Somnigender) .... Connected to being sleepy but not insomnia, might be hard to identify due to feeling sleepy.

SLIMEGENDER .... Multi-Gender feeling like all the genders are slimes mixed together in different amounts.

SLIWARMASIX .... Slightly warm, hovering slightly above other genders.

SMALLGENDER .... Half one gender, half Agender.

SMOKEUTIN .... Smoking, floating up between other genders smoking them out.

SNAKEGENDER .... Connected to snakes, might be like snakes.

SNARLBOY ♂ .... Masculine variation of Snarlgender.

SNARLGENDER .... Has sharp teeth, claws, things vicious and ferocious. {Snarlboy, Snarlgirl, Snarlnonbinary}

SNARLGIRL ♀ .... Feminine variation of Snarlgender.

SNARLNONBINARY .... Nonbinary variation of Snarlgender.

SNAILGENDER .... Connected to snails.

SNEKGENDER .... Small, wriggly, slithery.

SNICKERBARIC .... Connected to Snickers candy bars.

SNOWCORIC .... Connected to snow.

SNOWLEOPARDGENDER .... Cold, isolated, like snow leopards.

SOAPCORIC .... Connected to soap.

SOCUGENDER .... Connected to cutting bars of soap into cubes.

SOFT-STORMGENDER .... Connected to feeling safety, warmth, being home, fireplaces, blankets.

SOLISGENDER .... Bright, color yellow, joyful, sunny.

SOLVOGENDER .... A gender sailing away to another part of the gender, or like a swan, might eventually vanish.

SOMNIGENDER (see Sleepycoric)

SONNEAN ♂ .... Juparian, Plutoian.

SONNIAN .... Like a sonnet.

SOULGENDER .... Fluid, connected to Pixar movie Soul, might be lively, down to earth, determined, musical, strong, lonely, lost, confused, searching for purpose.

SOURYIC (Candyic, Canyic; see Candycoric)

SPACECORIC (Starfluid; see Astralgender)

SPARKLECORIC (Sparklegender) .... Connected to sparkly things, might be sparkly.

SPARKLEGENDER (see Sparklecoric)

SPECIESGENDER (see Felinegender)

SPOOKYGENDER .... Dark, scary.

SPOTGENDER .... A main gender with spots of other genders added to it.

SPRINGENDER .... Like a spinning wheel with multiple genders constantly spinning.

SPRIXYGENDER .... Three genders with Agender then Pangender then Neutrois.

SSmusihypic .... Connected to one's autistic based hyperfixation on Slim Shady the character created by rapper Eminem.

STAGMUN .... Fluid, no more than two genders, connected to lakes, like a lake or pond.

STARBOY ♂ .... Connected to boasting, cyberpunk, crime.

STARCORIC .... Connected to stars, either in the sky or famous people.

STARFLUID (Spacecoric; see Astralgender)

STARGENDER ♂♀ .... Including both masculinity and femininity yet being neutral but not androgynous.

STARIC (see Rockic)

STATICGENDER .... Like old fashioned TV static as is fuzzy, incomprehensible.

STEAMGENDER .... With multiple creative distinct parts, might have parts distributed to others.

STEAMUTIN .... Steamy, cleaning out other genders.

STELLAVIR ♂♀ .... Male with femininity being central to the identity.

STENDIC .... Connected to justice, morals, ethics, laws, might feel diety like.

STEPHONIC .... Connected to character Stephon Meyers of TV show Saturday Night Live, might be connected to clubbing, flirting, sexuality.

STIMGENDER .... Felt during stimming.

STITCHGENDER .... Chaotic, soft, connected to character Stitch of 2002 movie Lilo & Stich.

STONECORIC .... Connected to stones.

STOPTOGENDER .... A gender based on things one has seen.

STORECORIC .... Connected to stores.

STRATACOASTER .... Fluid, connected to rollercoasters over 400 feet tall, might have extreme highs, lows with abrupt transitions.

STRATOGENDER (see Lamingender)

STRESSFLUX .... Changing due to one's stress levels.

STRINGGENDER .... Think or thick or weak or strong, might be connected to ropes, string.

STROMAGENDER .... A gender filling up space around one's self.

SUBBOY ♂ .... Masculine variation of Nanogender.

SUBGENDER (see Nanogender)

SUBGIRL ♀ .... Feminine variation of Nanogender.

SUCUSBAONIC .... Bubbly, fizzy, connected to potions, bats, Halloween, color purple.

SUGARCORIC .... Connected to sugar.

SUIESOLUM .... Bright, connected to fire, color red.

SUNCORIC .... Connected to the sun.

SUPERAGENDER .... A gender going beyond gender and Agender identity.
{Supraboy, Supragirl}

SUPERIGENDER .... Connected to one's superiors, might act a certain way
towards superiors.

SUPERTASKGENDER .... A gender constantly revealing smaller and smaller
details about it.

SUPRABOY ♂ .... Masculine variation of Superagender.

SUPRAGIRL ♀ .... Feminine variation of Superagender.

SURFACEWEBGENDER .... Easy to find being very visible.

SURGENDER .... Being 100% one gender with part of another added to it.

SWEATERGENDER ♀ .... Wanting to feel soft, warm, safe, comfortable.

SWEETIEGENDER ♀ .... Connected to pastels, soft cute things, Japanese Anime,
stuffed animals.

SWIRLIC .... Feeling chaotic but in a positive and bouncy way, might be
connected to colors bright yellow, bright green.

SWORDGENDER .... A gender sharp to anyone trying to understand it other than
one's self, might be perceived differently that actually is.

SWUFEGENDER .... Being deceptively sweet, cute, innocent outside but inside
being dark, ruthless.

SYLVEGENDER .... A gender having evolved due to starting a relationship.

SYNESTHGENDER .... Connected to one's synesthesia, which is so intertwined
to one's gender the two can't be separated, might be fluid due to different
experiences.

TAFFYIC .... Connected to taffy.

TALIC .... Fierce, honorable, virtuous, warrior, other worldy.

TEALGENDER .... Connected to color teal.

TECHCORIC (Gendertech, Pantechnicum, Technogender; see Cybergender)

TECHGENDER .... A gender connected to computer coding.

TECHNOGENDER (Gendertech, Pantechnicum, Techcoric; see Cybergender)

TEDDYIC .... Connected to teddy bears.

TEENCORIC .... Connected to teens.

TEMNOSGEN .... Intensely felt, feeling cut out, reshaped due to dissatisfaction with it.

TEMNOVEZGENDER .... Feeling dark but not absent, like an empty abyss.

TENEBRAIC .... Felt vaguely like is in the shadows while feeling another gender with neither a comfortable gender. {Fem-Tenebraic, Masc-Tenebraic, Neut-Tenebraic}

TENEBRIC .... Cold, dark, smelling of moss, nature.

TENTGENDER .... Many genders staying comfortable in a tent protected from other genders.

TERAGENDER .... Very grand, marvelous, dangerous.

TERRACOTTAFLUID .... Fluid, like sand flowing to eventually harden into the static gender of Terracottani.

TERRACOTTANI .... Static gender being the result of the fluid gender Terracottafluid.

TERRAEAN (Terran, Terrean) ♂♀ .... Juparian, Lunettian, Plutoian.

TERRAN (Terrean; see Terraean) ♂♀

TERREAN (Terran; see Terraean) ♂♀

TERREGENDER .... Animalistic, otherworldly, connected to the ground.

TETAGENDER .... Cozy, safe, can be snuggled with.

THIRD GENDER (Enbie, Gender Nonconforming, Genderqueer, Gender Variant, Nonbinary, X-Gender; see Cogender)

TIGERGENDER .... Connected to tigers.

TIMORIC .... Connected to one's fear and anxiety due to intrusive thoughts on gender.

TODDLERIC .... Childish, giggly, rambunctious, like a toddler.

TOFFYIC .... Connected to toffee.

TONEGENDER .... Fluctuating between two colors on a gradient.

TOONCORIC .... Connected to cartoons.

TOONGENDER .... Connected to old cartoons, rubberhose style of cartooning, might be loose, stretchy, easily changing, two-dimensional.

TORGENDER .... Secure, anonymous feeling.

TOWNCORIC (see Citycoric)

TOXICCORIC .... Connected to toxic things.

TOYCORIC (Toyyic) .... Connected to toys.

TOYFREDIC .... Connected to character Toy Freddy of video game Five Nights At Freddy's, might be new, interesting, fresh, daring, dangerous, mechanical.

TOYGENDER ♂ .... Soft, playful, childlike, might have an affinity with one's toys from childhood, might feel like simplified toy compared to other genders.

TOYYIC (see Toycoric)

TPOC .... Trans, people of color.

TRAGENDER .... Being all of the gender spectrum.

TRANOGENDER .... Aimalistic, otherworldly, connected to flying.

TRANS (Transgender) .... A gender different than assigned gender at birth. {Transfeminine, Transfemme, Trans Man, Transmasc, Transmasculine, Trans Woman}

TRANSFEMININE (Transfemme, Trans Woman) ♀ .... Feminine variation of Trans.

TRANSFEMMASC ♀ .... Trans due to unassigned gender at birth, might be fluid.

TRANSFEMME (Trans Woman; see Transfeminine) ♀

TRANSGENDER (see Trans)

TRANS MAN (Transmasc, Transmasculine) ♂ .... Masculine variation of Trans.

TRANSMASC (Transmasculine; see Trans Man) ♂

TRANSMASCFEM ♂ .... Trans due to unassigned gender at birth, might be fluid.

TRANSMASCULINE (Transmasc; see Trans Man) ♂

TRANS WOMAN (Transfemme; see Transfeminine) ♀

TRAUATGENDER (Traumatagender, Traumatgender, Trautgender) .... A fluid gender created by intense trauma, might be felt while experiencing trauma, might be hard to describe.

TRAUMACORIC .... Connected to one's trauma.

TRAUMATAGENDER (Traumatgender, Trautgender; see Trauatgender)

TRAUMATGENDER (Traumatagender, Trautgender; see Trauatgender)

TRAUTGENDER (Traumatagender, Trautgender; see Trauatgender)

TRAVELCORIC .... Connected to travel.

TRIGENDER (Trigenderfluid) .... Three genders simultaneously or separately.

TRIGENDERFLUID (see Trigender)

TRI-VIR ♂ .... Three masculine genders simultaneously or separately.

TROFANNOLIAN .... Tropical, calming, might be connected to spring, oceans, beaches, seashells, rainbows.

TROOPILINEAN .... Tropical, colorful, windy, might be connected to summer, oceans, beaches, beach gift shops, surf music.

TROOPINNENIAN .... Tropical, like winter, might be connected to oceans, fish, beaches, seashells.

TROPSKIAN .... Tropical, free-spirted, loving, might be connected to fish, summer, oceans, beaches, surfing, surf music.

TUMTUM .... Jewish, Agender.

TWINKGENDER ♂ .... Connected to being a twink.

UISGENDER .... Multi-Gender not simultaneously, blurred, due to Dissociative Identity Disorder or mental disorder.

ULOSAGENDER .... Animalistic, otherworldly, connected to fairies.

ULTERGENDER .... Intersex, not identifying with Trans.

UMBRAGENDER .... Animalistic, otherworldly, connected to shadows.

UNASSIGNED-GENDER-AT-BIRTH (see AXAB)

UNBOY ♂ .... Masculine variation of Ungender.

UNDEADSOFT .... Connected to zombies, undead, might be due to mental disorder, might be comforting to one's self.

UNGENDER .... Being the negative of another gender. {Unboy, Ungirl}

UNGIRL ♀ .... Feminine variation of Ungender.

UNIBINARY .... Mixing both binary genders into one.

UNICORN (Earth Pony, Pegasus; see Ponygender)

UNIGENDER .... Feeling uniform with everyone else as nothing unique stands out about it.

URBANOX (Urbisluxgender) .... Peaceful, calm, chilly, like city lights at night, might be nostalgic, lonely, static, might seem to come on and off.

URBISGENDER .... Like a city with many small parts working together with infinite things to discover.

URBISLUXGENDER (see Urbanox)

UTRINQUEGENDER .... A gender with both Trans and Cisgender experiences.

UTTUVIRUAN ♂ .... Calming, small, connected to autumn, pumpkins, cinnamon, candles, might be like cold October days, festive smells, autumn rain.

VACAGENDER (Intergender, Intergenderless; see Ingender)

VAERMIC .... Changes based on type of dreams.

VAGUEBOY ♂ .... Masculine variation of Nebgender.

VAGUEGENDER (see Nebgender)

VAGUEGIRL♀ .... Feminine variation of Nebgender.

VALENTINECORIC .... Connected to Valentine's Day.

VALGEIAN .... Connected to color white.

VAMPCORIC .... Connected to vampires.

VAPOGENDER .... Like smoke as has shallow feeling with further investigation eventually disappears leaving no gender.

VAPORWAVIC .... Connected to Vaporwave music and culture.

VASEGENDER .... Feeling fragile but holding something beautiful.

VELVETIC .... Connected to velvet, soft things, linen, blankets.

VENERESFLUID .... Fluid, slowly descends into area of one's gender being deep, warm, small, developing into Genderveneres.

VENNGENDER .... Two genders overlapping to create an entirely new gender.

VENUSARIAN ♀ .... Nonbinary with changing intensities of soft celestial feminine energy.

VERANGENDER .... Appearing to change the moment it is identified, might not actually change.

VERMIL ♂ .... Nonbinary with traditional masculine presentation.

VERSUOGENDER .... Two or more genders blended together at their edges but remaining mostly separate.

VERWARMASIX .... Warm, hovering high above other genders, might flare up into other genders destroying them.

VESPERTINUSFLUID .... Calm, fluid, flows into darkness deep inside itself to bring genders back out incorporating them into itself.

VESTIGENDER .... Blankets a stronger gender but is the only visible gender.

VESTIGIBAONIC .... In trace amounts barely revealing itself.

VEUSIAN (see Juparettian) ♂♀

VHSGENDER .... Old, enjoyable, familiar.

VIBRAGENDER .... Static gender occasionally changing to another before stabilizing again with original gender.

VIBROGENDER .... Feeling like it vibrates.

VICTORIAGENDER .... Connected to Victorian Era.

VIDEGENDER (Aestheticgender, Aesthetigender; see Aesthetgender)

VIDEOGENDER .... Feeling too robotic to be described in human terms.

VILENGENDER .... Connected to villains or feeling villainous.

VILLAGECORIC .... Connected to villages.

VINCIANGENDER (Gaygender; see Achilleangender) ♂

VINTAGECORIC .... Connected to vintage things.

VINTAGEGENDER .... Connected to vintage objects of 1920 to 1980, or a gender triggered when remembering something nostalgic.

VIOLABOY ♂ .... Masculine variation of Violagender.

VIOLAGENDER .... Calming, open-minded, connected to oceans and sky simultaneously via identifying with oceans when weather is colder and identifying with the sky when weather is warmer. {Violaboy, Violagirl, Violanonbinary}

VIOLAGIRL ♀ .... Feminine variation of Violagender.

VIOLANONBINARY .... Nonbinary variation of Violagender.

VIRFIDEM ♂ .... Christian, Trans.

VIRGENDER .... Being practically Agender but becoming present when having a gender becomes too stressful and difficult.

VIRILIGENDER ♂ .... Nonbinary Trans-men who find it harmful associating with men.

VIRISOLUM .... Connected to nature, health, the sun, color green.

VISIGENDER (Visuogender; see Enigender)

VISUOGENDER (Visigender; see Enigender)

VITANTI .... Feeling inanimate or stagnant due to mental disorder, might feel like never having been alive.

VITIUMGENDER .... Connected to one's physical or mental disability or chronic illness.

VOCIGENDER .... Weak or hollow.

VOID (Voidgender; see Gendervoid)

VOIDGENDER (Void; see Gendervoid)

VOLOGENDER .... Airy, wispy, barely existent, might eventually fade out of existence.

VOREGENDER .... Warm, all encompassing, comforting.

VULVULGENDER .... A gender turning old genders into new genders.

VURILIC .... Connected to computer viruses.

WALLGENDER .... A gender sometimes separated from other genders, might not understand genders other than one's own. {Wallboy, Wallgirl}

WALLBOY ♂ .... Masculine variation of Wallgender.

WALLGIRL ♀ .... Feminine variation of Wallgender.

WANDERLUST GENDER .... Sometimes eerie, like a labyrinth being impossible to navigate, easy to get lost in, might not cause anxiety.

WARMCOLOREN .... Connected to warm colors.

WARPGENDER .... Connected to the Warped Forest biome in video game Minecraft, might be foggy, cool, loneliness feeling, silent.

WARRIORGENDER .... Connected to book series Warriors by Erin Hunter.

WAVIC .... Connected to Wave electronica music and culture.

WATERMELETYPE ♀ .... Feminine gender reclaiming negative stereotypes around women of color.

WEIRDGIRL ♀ .... Binary girl in a weird way.

WELLGENDER .... Deep, dark, infinite, might be connected to water.

WILDGENDER .... Connected to Wild Card from game Uno, might be unpredictably fluid or static.

WINDOWGENDER .... Fluid, transparent, like the space between the glass and the screen of the window.

WINGCORIC (Wingphinaec) .... Connected to wings, or having wings, or wanting wings.

WINGPHINAEC (see Wingcoric)

WINTERCORIC .... Connected to cold, snow, winter holidays.

WIRELESSGENDER .... Connected to wireless communication, internet.

WITCHCORIC .... Connected to witches, might be connected to Halloween.

WITHERIC .... Connected to character Withered Freddy of video game Five Nights At Freddy's, might be worn down, sneaky, dangerous, watchful, mechanical.

WOODCORIC .... Connected to wood, might be connected to woodworking, might be connected to trees.

WORLDOFENEF .... Connected to video game Five Nights At Freddy's World, might only be felt when playing game.

WORSHIPGENDER .... Connected to religious worship.

XENOGENDER (Quasixenic see Aliagender

XENOIRGENDER .... Connected to Emo and Goth music and cultures.

XEUPHOGENDER .... Feeling like the party is peaking, the night at its darkest, the energy at its highest.

XICONGENDER .... Animalistic, otherworldly, connected to poison or poisonous things.

XIN (Xingender) .... Being both Xenine gender, not Xenine.

XINGENDER (see Xin)

XENBIE (Xenby) .... Being both Xenine, nonbinary.

XENBY (see Xenbie)

XENINE .... Not having a strong sense of one's gender but only vague ideas, feelings, descriptions.

X-GENDER (Enbie, Gender Nonconforming, Genderqueer, Gender Variant, Nonbinary, Third Gender; see Cogender)

XIRL ♀ .... Connected to some part of being a girl but not feeling completely a girl, wanting nonbinary and neutral sounding gender identity to avoid associating with traditional definitions of girl.

XOY ♂ .... Connected to some part of being a boy but not feeling completely a boy, wanting a nonbinary and neutral sounding gender identity to avoid associating with traditional definitions of boy.

XUMGENDER (Pendogender; see Pendo-Agender)

YELLOWGENDER .... Connected with color yellow.

ZACHAR ♂ .... Jewish, assigned male at birth, Cisgender.

ZAUYGENDER .... Connected to feelings of not possessing a soul, not existing, not being alive, might be due to mental disorders.

ZELOSGENDER .... A gender causing jealousy when others use the same label, might change labels, might be due to needing attention.

ZENGEN .... Connected to Zen Buddhism.

ZENITHIC .... A gender which tries to change with other genders, other worldly energy.

ZIGGYSTARDUSTGENDER (see Burlesgender)

ZODIACGENDER .... Connected to astrology.

ZOMBIECORIC .... Connected to zombies, might be decayed, dark.

NOTES

NOTES

www.ingramcontent.com/pod-product-compliance
Lightning Source LLC
Chambersburg PA
CBHW051831250726

48659CB00005B/1789